IN THE END—
THE BEGINNING

Jürgen Moltmann

IN THE END—
THE BEGINNING

The Life of Hope

Translated by
Margaret Kohl

FORTRESS PRESS
Minneapolis

IN THE END—THE BEGINNING
The Life of Hope

First Fortress Press edition 2004

Cover art: Falaise d'Aval at Sunset (Normandy, France); Timothy McCarthy / Art Resource, NY. Used with permission.
Cover design: Jessica Thoreson

ISBN: 8006-3656-2

Manufactured in the U.S.A.

Contents

PART TWO:
IN MY END IS MY BEGINNING

PART THREE:
O BEGINNING WITHOUT ENDING . . .

whatsoever to do with the end, whether it be the end of this life, the end of history, or the end of the world. Christian expectation is about the beginning: the beginning of true life, the beginning of God's kingdom, and the beginning of the new creation of all things into their enduring form. The ancient wisdom of hope says: 'The last things are as the first.' So God's great promise in the last book of the Bible, the book of Revelation, is: 'Behold, I make all things new' (21.5). In the light of this ultimate horizon we read the Bible as the book of God's promises and the hopes of men and women – indeed the hopes of everything created; and from the remembrances of their future we find energies for the new beginning.

'In the end, the beginning': in my book *The Coming of God. Christian Eschatology* (1995; ET 1996) I looked at this funda-mental affirmation in the different contexts in which the future is awaited: the personal contexts, the political contexts, and the cosmic ones. In this little doctrine of hope I am concentrating on the personal experiences of life in which we search for new beginnings and find them. If the last is not the end but the new beginning, we have no need to stare fascinated at the end of life. We can start with life's beginning. The birth of life precedes its death. In the miracle of a child's being-born, there is 'a magic', as the poet Hermann Hesse wrote, which points beyond the experiences of life's finitude, its failures, disappointments and defeats. It is not the magic of our wishes and fantasies. It is the magic of originality, of firstness. Wherever in our lives we come close to the origin, and become originals again ourselves, we experience new beginnings. The living God always calls to life, whether we are born or whether we die, whether we can begin or whether we have come to the end. His nearness makes us living, always and everywhere.

The three parts of this doctrine of hope correspond to the three beginnings in our own lives: birth – rebirth – resurrection.

In the first part I shall be looking at childhood and youth – that is to say, the beginnings of life in terms of time. With every child something new comes into the world. So for us the word 'childhood' has the resonances of an open future, a future full of everything possible; and it is often used as a parable of hope for the fullness of life. The word 'youth' is similar. 'The future

Introduction

In my end is my beginning': so T. S. Eliot concluded his poem *East Coker*, and that conclusion gave me the title for this book. I have chosen it as a way of expressing the power of the Christian hope, for Christian hope is the power of resurrection from life's failures and defeats. It is the power of life's rebirth out of the shadows of death. It is the power for the new beginning at the point where guilt has made life impossible. The Christian hope is all these things because it is spirit from the Spirit of the resurrection of the betrayed, maltreated and forsaken Christ. Through his divine raising from the dead, Christ's hope-less end became his true beginning. If we remember that, we shall not give ourselves up, but shall expect that in every end a new beginning lies hidden. Yet we shall only become capable of new beginnings if we are prepared to let go of the things that torment us, and the things we lack. If we search for the new beginning, it will find us.

Some people think that the Bible has to do with the terrors of the apocalypse, and that the apocalypse is 'the end of the world'. The end, they believe, will see the divine 'final solution' of all the unsolved problems in personal life, in world history, and in the cosmos. Apocalyptic fantasy has always painted God's great final Judgement on the Last Day with flaming passion: the good people will go to heaven, the wicked will go to hell, and the world will be annihilated in a storm of fire. We are all familiar, too, with images of the final struggle between God and Satan, Christ and the Antichrist, Good and Evil in the valley of Armageddon – images which can be employed so usefully in political friend-enemy thinking.

These images are apocalyptic, but are they also Christian? No, they are not; for Christian expectation of the future has nothing belongs to the young' we say, and because of that modern adults want to escape the ageing process and remain 'forever young'. But couldn't it really be the reverse that is true – that it is the prospects of the future which make us young, however old we may be in terms of years?

In the second part I shall go into the courage for living which hope quickens in us, so that we can get up again out of failures, disappointments and defeats, and begin life afresh. No one is perfect, and few people succeed in achieving an unbroken continuity in their lives. Again and again we come up against limits, and experience the failure of our plans for life, the fragmentary nature of our good beginnings and, not least, the guilt which makes life impossible for us. The essential thing in experiences of life like this is the new beginning. If a child falls over it is no bad thing, because it then learns to get up again. Christian faith is faith in the resurrection, and the resurrection is literally just that: rising up again. It gives us the strength to get up, and the creative freedom to begin something once more in the midst of our ongoing history, something fresh. '*Incipit vita nova*' – a new life begins. That is the truly revolutionary power of hope. It is revolutionary because it is innovative. With it, we break down the compulsive need for success. With it, we leave behind us the fatalism of non-success. 'Christians are the eternal beginners', wrote Franz Rosenzweig. And that is the best thing that can ever be said about believers, lovers and the hopeful.

It is only in the third part that I shall turn to what are known as 'the last things', which when they touch on personal life are called death – judgement – eternal life. Is there a life after death? Is there a community between the living and the dead? What does mourning mean, and what is consolation? We are awaited. But what awaits us? How ought we to imagine God's Judgement and 'the life of the world to come'?

The different chapters have grown out of lectures held during general courses at the university of Tübingen, at the Protestant lay assemblies in Germany (the *Kirchentage*), and at secular conferences. They are intended for a wide readership, so I have avoided technical theological terms and numerous quotations, and have tried to find words for my own personal conviction. Nothing is presupposed except interest in the subject; so instead of theological terminology I have preferred to turn to lines of poetry or verses of hymns, which express the same thing in a more memorable way.

Jürgen Moltmann
Tübingen

PART ONE

THERE IS A MAGIC
IN EVERY BEGINNING

✦•✦

PART ONE

THERE IS A MAGIC
IN EVERY BEGINNING

➤•◄

I

The Promise of the Child

'There is a magic in every beginning', wrote Hermann Hesse. What does this mean, if we think about the beginning of every human life? In order to grasp this more clearly, let us look at the biblical concept of promise. A divine promise is the promise of a future which God is going to bring about. When God promises something he is bound to keep his promise, for his own sake and for the sake of his glory. His whole being is faithfulness. That is why we human beings can trust him and can believe what he promises. Abraham and Sarah offer the primal image of this kind of trust, for according to Genesis 12 they left everything in response to God's promise that he would make of them a great people and a blessing for all generations of human beings. The departure of Abraham and Sarah from their home country, and the wanderings that followed, show that a divine promise doesn't just point forward to some far-off future, which we have to wait for; the promised future is already present in the promise itself, and mobilizes the people concerned through the hope it awakens. The biblical stories have made us familiar with divine promises of this kind in verbal form, but we find God's promises in the form of events too, events which point beyond themselves, like the miracle of the Reed Sea, which saved Israel from its persecutors. We meet divine promises which have taken human form among the prophets. And from the psalms we also perceive that everything that God has created points beyond itself to the Creator and to the future of his glory, for which it has been created. Everything that is and lives, holds within itself this 'magic' of promise and points beyond itself, as the beginning of something greater.

In the biblical stories, from early on we find 'the child of promise'. We shall see what this orientation towards the future has to say to us in a world of the ancestor cult, of patriarchies and matriarchies. We shall then see how this special promise of the messianic child who is to redeem the world is reflected in the context of life in general, and shall try to discover what 'the promise of the child' means for all of us.

'To us a child is born', proclaims the prophet Isaiah to his people who are 'walking in darkness' (Isa. 9.6, 9.2). The destruction of their country, the expulsion from their homeland, forced labour in Babylon: a black eclipse of God had fallen on God's people. With the announcement of the birth of the messianic child and his reign of peace 'without end', the prophet gives hope once more to the stricken people. The yoke of their burden and the rod of their oppressors will disappear. The year 587 brought a catastrophic end, with the capture of Jerusalem and the deportation into exile, but a new beginning is coming, a beginning as full of new possibilities as a child that has just been born. So 'the child of promise' becomes the symbol for the future of life, in contrast to the sufferings of the present. And in this way it also becomes the pledge of God's faithfulness: he will find his forsaken people and bring them home.

'In every child the messiah can be born', says a Jewish proverb. So every child deserves respect. It is encompassed by the magic of the messianic hope. At Christmas, Christians celebrate the festival of the birth of the Redeemer in 'the child in the manger' in Bethlehem. What are we really doing then? We are celebrating the encounter with the almighty God in the weak and helpless child Jesus. But this presupposes a tremendous proceeding: the Creator of heaven and earth, whom even the heaven of heavens cannot contain, becomes so humble and small that in this child Jesus he is beside us and lives among us. The theology of the early Church said that in this event God 'became man' – became human. But the mystery really begins with God's *becoming a child*. The great, all-comprehensive rule of God begins as *this child's* rule of peace. The gospel of Christ is profoundly engraved by the gospel about children: 'Whoever receives a child receives me' and: 'Unless you become like children . . .', for the kingdom of God is theirs.

This religious orientation towards the child of promise and

peace is not merely Jewish and Christian. It was familiar to the prophecy and philosophy of the ancient world too.[1] Virgil's famous Fourth Eclogue, which Christians later adopted for themselves, prophesies the birth of the redeeming child:

> Now the Virgin returns, the reign of Saturn returns; now a new generation descends from heaven on high. Only do you, pure Lucina, smile on the birth of the child, under whom the iron brood shall at last cease and a golden race spring up throughout the world! Your own Apollo now is king . . . See how the world bows its massive dome – earth and expanse of sea and heaven's depth! See how all things rejoice in the age that is at hand.[2]

And even earlier the supposedly obscure philosopher Heraclitus wrote:

> Lifetime is a child playing, moving pieces in a (backgammon?) game:
> Kingly power (or: the kingdom) is in the hands of a child.
>
> (Fragment 52)[3]

Heraclitus means that behind the becoming and passing away of phenomena in nature and history, the guiding hand of a wise king is evident in the form of a carefree, playing child.

'The reign of a child': the divine is not just the primordially old. It is at the same time the archetypally childlike. The world is like a child's game, and in the child what is divine comes to appearance.

If we see the particular birth of the child of promise as mirroring the promise of children in general, we can cry with the Romantic poet Clemens Brentano, 'What a mystery is a child!' In his poem Brentano traces the pattern of this mystery, seeing in it a triple-stranded bond between our relation to God as his children, the birth of the Redeemer as a child, and the special relationship to all children forged for us through the child Jesus.[4]

The Mystery of the Child: Some Perspectives

Children grow up in the world of adults, and experience themselves in the way adults think is appropriate for a child.[5] From what angle do we perceive the mystery hidden in every child? The way parents and teachers talk about a child is different from the way the child talks about itself, and different again from the way adults remember their own childhood. According to the perspective we choose, we see the childhood of educational theory, the child's own childhood, or a childhood with a future ahead of it. It must always be remembered that here for the most part we are talking about the secure middle-class childhood familiar to us. We are not talking about the blighted childhood of the street children in Bucharest, or of the children forced into prostitution in Bangkok, or the child labourers in India, or the child soldiers in Africa. But if we take the three perspectives we have mentioned, what is childhood?

1. From the viewpoint of parents and teachers, childhood is of course on the one hand an inherently good and meaningful stage in life; but from another and more important aspect it is a state which has to be surmounted, through the child's own development, and through upbringing on the adult side, an upbringing which is designed to meet the expectations of society as a whole. When all is said and done, parents have to 'bring up' their children, as we say, so that 'they can make something of themselves', and are able to master an adult life in which they make their own decisions. Both these aspects have to be taken into account and balanced against one another. Parents ought to play with their children because they enjoy them just as they are. So they shouldn't just play 'educational' games, like Scrabble or Monopoly. They should play hide and seek or football as well. And yet parents are bound to look beyond the present childhood of their children, towards their possible future in the adult world, so that they can give the children bearings and guidelines. If they are to do this they must also have the courage to be adult themselves, and not to dress like teenagers, or talk like children.

Ever since the beginning of the middle-class era, with its faith in progress, belief in progress has dominated the upbringing of children too. Childhood now came to be understood only as the preliminary stage on the way to the full personhood of the adult. This was typified by the often-heard question: 'Well, young man, what are you going to be when you grow up?' Boys were trained to be in command of themselves, and to have control of their bodies, preferably through toys that have to do with fighting, hitting and shooting. Dolls prepared girls for their future role as mothers. In this way the child's own future was pressed into the pre-existing moulds of the adult world. From this perspective, childhood was merely a personhood still to be developed. The model of complete personhood was then supposed to be the adult between the ages of 25 and 60, preferably the man 'in his prime', as the phrase went.

If we apply for a job, we are obliged to write a curriculum vitae, an account of our previous career. But the world *curriculum* originally meant a race. So according to the curriculum vitae the whole of life from the cradle to the grave is a race from one stage to the next. Learning is supposed to be 'life-long'. But what are we really learning for?

In the middle-class family, the all-important thing was social advancement from one generation to the next. With that in mind, one dressed 'according to one's position in life', but lived 'above one's circumstances' and saved by eating at home 'beneath one's station'. But is childhood too a matter of 'advancement'? Is it really no more than a still undeveloped human condition which has to be surmounted? The great historian Leopold von Ranke already protested against the credulous faith in progress which reduced the past to a mere preliminary stage on the way to the future. He maintained, conversely, that 'Every age is immediate to God, for in every age the Divine desires to realize itself, and is unable to show itself in its entirety in any single era.' This is also true of age in the personal sense: children and young people, adults and the old, find the meaning of their lives in whatever is their own present at any given time. Every lived moment has an eternal significance and already constitutes a fulfilled life. For fulfilled life is not measured by the number of years that have been lived through, or spent in one way or another. It is measured according to the depth of lived experience. Even a child who dies young has had a fulfilled life. Every child has a right to its own present, and the life fulfilled in that particular present must be respected by parents and teachers. It must not be sacrificed on the altar of progress.

Janusz Korczak, the director of the Jewish orphanage in Warsaw, who accompanied his children to the death camp, identified some fundamental children's rights, which must be respected by everyone who loves a child. Among these are (1) the child's right to the present day; and (2) the child's right to be as it is.[6] These fundamental rights also represent a claim to human rights on the part of children, so that infringement of these rights can be brought before the courts.

Of course to say that childhood is intrinsically meaningful, and that every moment is a fulfilment, is also wishful thinking on the part of adults: it is what they hope for their children. Adults who have become slaves of their over-organized time like to dream about those wonderful childhood years, which were so carefree and without set purpose. But as a corrective to an up-bringing which presses forward with the aim of rapid progress, this dream is a valuable utopia. What we need, whether we are children, adolescents, adults or the old, is a balance between experience of the present and expectation of the future, between the fulfilled moment and the beginning of a new day.

2. What childhood means for children themselves is surely bound to remain an almost impenetrable mystery for us adults. When the child was still a child it hardly knew that it was a child. It is the encounter with grown-ups which first makes a child aware that it is a child. But then the grown-up viewpoint enters the child's awareness. Adults themselves only become conscious of their own childhood as they actually experienced it when they are no longer children. Every perception requires distance, and self-perception requires a degree of alienation as well. I believe that childhood is limited and defined by the fact that children have ceased to be in the safekeeping of the mother's womb but are still unable to be independent. On the one hand they feel the dependence, the nightly terrors, the helpless fears of some overwhelming power, and the empty days when they complain 'I don't know what to do'. We remember how small we were, and how tall our father, and how omniscient our mother, and how ignorant we ourselves were, and how the bigger children could already do everything that we couldn't. On the other hand

we experienced everything and did everything for the first time, full of curiosity and the joy of discovery. With boundless astonishment we followed the flight of a fly, and perplexed our parents with unanswerable 'whys'. We could play in complete self-forgetfulness and react spontaneously with laughter or tears. The darkness of the lived moment was often still very dark, and became no lighter either before or afterwards. Of course before we went to school we 'just played' – that, at least, is the way the grown-ups saw it, and we adopted their viewpoint for ourselves. We have to respect the inner viewpoint of a child during its childhood as its own secret. All our analyses lead only to projections on to the child of our own ideas, and destroy its freedom.

3. How do adults view their own childhood, and how do they discover the child in themselves? 'I swore to remain eternally young' was the title Johannes Kessler, the German Emperor William II's court preacher, gave his once-famous book. Today the slogan is terser: 'Forever young!' Dreams of this kind are regressive, and prevent many adults from accepting their advancing age. Sometimes, of course, people seem to need regressions like this, for example during the carnival season in Germany and elsewhere. In 1999 the carnival song of the year in Cologne ran:

With carnival each year
The child in me appears.

Regressions during 'the mad days' (as this time-out is called) are not just childish. They are healthy too if they let off the steam bottled up during the disciplined working lives which adults are compelled to lead.

People sometimes idealize childhood and youth – if they find themselves in a midlife crisis perhaps, or, with half their lives gone, suddenly realize that they no longer have many more options, because the important decisions in life have already been irrevocably made. If they feel that they have 'missed the boat', they idealize the beginnings, when everything was still possible. Then childhood appears as a time of unlimited opportunities and as the potential inherent in every beginning. 'Do not despise the dreams of your youth', says the Marquis von Posa in Schiller's *Don Carlos*. Childhood and youth are then transfigured with the daybreak colours of the dawn of life; for of course more is always inherent in our beginnings than we are able to realize, often under adverse circumstances. If we think back to our early years, and remember everything that we might have become, what emerges is something like a childhood seen with the eyes of the future. Then we see ourselves as we originally were. We feel the security of the carefree child – we again experience life as a mystery, marvellous and full of riddles – we are possessed by the innocence of life's pure beginnings. That is why children are for us always 'innocent', even though we have no way of judging whether this is in fact true. That is why we see in their eyes no evil but only dreaming purity.

This imagined childlike innocence, this image of the pure beginning, this world of unlimited possibilities – all this makes childhood the image of hope. But in this childhood seen through the eyes of the future we see in the beginnings the source of life. And when we search for 'the child in us' it is because we long to open this wellspring in ourselves once more.

The Messianic Child

The child whose birth and future reign of peace is announced by the prophet Isaiah in chapter 11 is the Son of David. He comes from the tribe of David, and is invested with the dignity of the king chosen by God. David once conquered Jerusalem and achieved an enduring place for the Ark of the Covenant; and similarly the future Son of David will redeem Israel from captivity and bring it to the new Jerusalem. In him the prophet Nathan's ancient promise to David will be fulfilled: 'I will raise up your offspring after you, who shall come forth from your body, and I will establish his kingdom *for ever*' (2 Sam. 7.12f.). The Son of David who is promised is to be Israel's hoped-for messiah-king. The expectations placed in him burst apart all human limits: he will raise up the poor in the land, he will bring justice and righteousness into the world of the nations, and, not least, will establish peace between human beings and animals. The wolf will lie down by the lamb, little children will play with snakes, and lions will eat straw like the oxen (Isa. 11.1–9).

It is true that this hope for the messianic child of peace grew up at what has been called Israel's zero hour, the Babylonian captivity; but it is nonetheless part of Israel's traditions of hope from the beginning. With God's promise to Abraham and Sarah, orientation towards the future in history took the place of the forces of origin for Israel. Children were not integrated into the potency of their origins with the help of the ancestor cult. Instead the different generations took their bearings from the children, seeing in them the guarantee of the faithfulness of the God of their promise. The messiah who was to deliver them must come from the children. The biblical 'God of hope' (Rom. 15.13) is always a God of children too. We might say, with a degree of exaggeration, that in this way the messianism of the child replaces in principle both patriarchy and matriarchy, the rule of fathers and mothers. I say 'in principle' advisedly, for historically this was not the case. Historically, we are told, 'to us a child is born, to us a son is given' (Isa. 9.6); and that means inheritance through the male line. But if only a son can carry on the tradition, and in this case be the bearer of hope, then sons must be born to families and daughters must be avoided. And we know to what degree Confucius and the age-old ancestor cult made of the countries of Asia countries of 'dead daughters'.

But there is another messianic tradition as well in the scriptures of Jews and Christians, and this identifies the child of promise not as son but as daughter. This is the Wisdom tradition. In the book of Proverbs, chapter 8, the Wisdom of God, *hokma*, is called 'the daughter of God', the daughter who was beside God before creation:

When he established the heavens . . .
When he made firm the skies above . . .
When he assigned to the sea its limit:
Then I was beside him like a master workman;
And I was daily his delight, playing before him always,
playing in his inhabited world,
and delighting in the children of men.

Wisdom, the divine daughter, resembles Heraclitus's aeon: she is the wise child playing with the world. Later Israelite traditions fused the two figures of hope, making out of the messiah and wisdom the Wisdom Messiah.[7] If we understand wisdom not just as a human virtue but in the first place as a presence of God in creation, then we understand why Jesus is presented in the New Testament both as Israel's messiah and as the Wisdom of creation, so that the Christ mystery is both male and female. When the Gospel of John calls the divine mystery of Jesus the Logos, the Word of God, Sophia, the Wisdom of God is meant too. Jesus is the incarnate Sophia, Jesus is the incarnate Logos – both Sophia and Logos given human form.[8]

So in the circumstances of our own day we can say at Christmas with the same joy as before: 'To us a child is born, to us a daughter is given!'

Jesus and Children: The Revaluation of Values

Christian culture has made us all familiar with the picture of the Madonna – the portrait of the single parent – with the child Jesus in her arms. It is of course a touching picture. But what is much more important is the revolutionary way Jesus treated children, as the Gospels describe it. Here Jesus is not the gentle 'friend of little children' painted by the sentimental middle classes in the nineteenth century. We know that in the world of ancient Rome children didn't count for much. That doesn't mean that parents didn't love their children. But the legal status of children was slight. Like women and slaves, children were the property of the head of the household, and could be sold or exposed, a fate to which girls particularly were subject. The Greek words for child and slave have the same root. Even in the New Testament words like 'childlike' or 'children' are used disparagingly (1 Cor. 14.20; Luke 7.32). This makes the high rank that Jesus gives children all the more remarkable.[9]

'Let the children come to me, do not hinder them; for to such belongs the kingdom of God' (Mark 10.14; Matt. 19.14; Luke 18.16). The male disciples think that the children are simply too immature, and want to keep them away from their master. But Jesus dismisses their objection, embraces the children and blesses them, calling them blessed because they already possess the kingdom of God which he proclaims and embodies. To be confident

of this can be a comfort if children die. Like the poor in the Sermon on the Mount, children are Jesus' fellow citizens in the kingdom. Why? How have they deserved it? The kingdom, and hence the nearness of God, belongs to children for the very reason that they have done nothing for it. They are given the kingdom just as they are given their birth. Looked at the other way round, this means: the kingdom of God doesn't come to the higher echelons of human society and at the spearhead of progress, among the achievers and the powerful. It comes to the unimportant people at the bottom of this world's social ladder. That turns our normal human scale of values upside down: the last shall be first. But if the kingdom of God comes to the people 'down there' in the world, then the people 'at the top' lose their religious legitimation. The 'woe' to the rich belongs to the beatitude which calls the poor blessed; and similarly the beatitude calling the children blessed goes on to curse the people who hurt or violate them: 'If any of you put a stumbling block before one of these little ones, it would be better for you if a millstone were fastened around your neck and you were drowned in the depth of the sea' (Matt.18.6). If God's kingdom comes to this world through the poor and through children, then the same is true of God's judgement.

'*Whoever receives one such child in my name receives me, and whoever receives me receives the one who sent me*' (Mark 9.37) – and that means God himself. Through these identifications, Jesus makes children his representatives in society. Just as God is in Christ by virtue of Christ's messianic mission, so Christ is present in every child. Anyone who 'receives' a child receives God. That sounds as if children have a divine dignity. There is a difference between the active mission of Christ and the passive expectation of Christ. 'He who hears you hears me' is said to the adult disciples. 'He who receives them receives me' is said about the children. Christ is present on both sides.

'*Unless you become like children, you will never enter the kingdom of God*' (Matt. 18.3). This is Jesus' answer to the disciples' typically male question: 'Who is the greatest in the kingdom of God?' The person who wants to be the greatest must be the servant of all, must 'become humble like this child' (18.4). This means, surely, that we should accept ourselves not in our strength but in our weakness before God, not in our pride over our maturity, but in the humility of being a child. We enter God's kingdom when we receive it like a child: with empty hands. We don't have to become children again – that would be childish – but we should become 'like a child'. That is a comparison. Children are close to the kingdom of God not because they have characteristics which adults have lost – innocence, perhaps, or purity, or naivety. It is rather that the kingdom of God is close to them because God loves them, embraces them and blesses them. Anyone who experiences the nearness of the living God in the fellowship of Jesus becomes like a child: life is born again and begins afresh. The later expression for this is sonship or daughterhood of God.

What new values does Jesus' gospel about children give us?

In the Christian sphere we assume that with Jesus the Christ, Israel's messiah and the saviour of the nations has come into the world – that is to say, 'the child of promise'. This has certain consequences:

1. There is no longer any *need* for a son to be given to us. We no longer wait for the messiah in our male descendants. So the religious privileges of fathers and sons come to an end, and hence the legal privileges too. Daughters are equally endowed with the Spirit and receive the same baptism (Gal. 3.28). The right to inherit the future of God's kingdom is given to sons and daughters equally. So daughters and sons are the bearers of hope for humanity.
2. There is now really no longer any *need* for a child to be born so that it may be the bearer of the coming kingdom of peace, for with Christ this kingdom has already come into the world. So lovers no longer have to justify their relationship or their marriage on the grounds that its purpose is the procreation of children. There is no religious duty to have a child. But there is no right to a child either. Children are a gift of God and a joy for their parents, who respect their children in their own right as God's children.
3. There is in principle no longer any *need* for men and women to marry, once the compulsion to marry for the sake of per-petuating God's people and humanity as such no long applies.

Voluntary celibacy and voluntary virginity were also possible ways of Christian existence from the beginning, and by no means merely deficient ways of living.

4. But, on the other hand, with this gospel the light of hope rests on every new-born child. Every child brings into the world a new beginning of life, and grows into the dawning fullness of the life to come. If children are God's creation, they are also created for this future of his creation. They must be viewed and accepted in this transcendent dimension, in which they themselves exist and in which they can develop. A society which presses its children into the existing patterns of the adult world is robbing itself of its own future. With every child something new comes into the world, and from these renewals of life we can expect something for the hoped-for kingdom of peace and fulfilled life. Children are different, said Maria Montessori rightly, and cited Emerson, who maintained that the child is the eternal messiah who returns again and again among fallen men and women, in order to lead us into the kingdom of heaven.[10]

Hope Which Shines Out for Everyone in Childhood

The birth of every child is a new beginning of life. With every child something new comes into the world. What do these beginnings point to? What does this new thing herald? Ernst Bloch concluded his great philosophy of hope with the sentence: '... Thus something comes into the world which shines out to all of us in childhood, and where no one has as yet ever been: home.'[11] Philosophically he called this home – or home country (*Heimat*) – of human beings 'the home of identity' in which human beings so come to themselves that all alienations cease. The essence of existence, which now only ferments or presses forward in darkness, will then emerge completely. Life will be whole and complete. That is a paraphrase for the fullness of life, the life which is also called eternal. For Bloch, *Heimat,* the home country, is the longed-for goal of hope in its totality: home in nature for human beings, a transfiguration of the world, a rebirth to the new all-comprehending life. With this symbol he describes

hope in its totality, beginning with 'real democracy' and ending
with 'the kingdom of God'.

How can this home country be 'something which shines out to
everyone in childhood, but where no one has as yet ever been'?
This reaches out beyond all the familiar images and feelings
about home we know. For Bloch the term *Heimat* is part of
Israel's history of hope: hope is the promised land of the fulfilled
divine promise. The home country means that God dwells
among human beings and human beings dwell with God. God's
covenant promise to Israel is 'I will dwell among them and they
shall be my people'. If God 'dwells' among human beings, and if
human beings share that dwelling with him, then that home
country has been reached where no one has as yet ever been but
which nevertheless shines out for everyone in childhood. According to the New Testament, this is God's final promise: 'Behold,
the dwelling of God is with men. He will dwell with them, and
they shall be his people' (Rev. 21.3). Then the earth will be newly
created so as to become God's dwelling place. Then human
beings too will be born again, so as to find their home country
in God. God and human beings will be indwellable for one
another.

These mutual indwellings of God and human beings are not
remote speculations. They are the daily experiences of love. 'He
who abides in love abides *in God*, and God abides *in him*' (1
John 4.16). That is 'the darkness of the lived moment', as Bloch
calls this mystical instant – and that he really does mean it mystically is shown by his early writings, for there he could still call
this darkness of the lived moment 'the darkness of the lived
God'.[12] Children live spontaneously and unconsciously in the
darkness of the lived God. What shines out for them in their
childhood and awakens the longing for that home of identity is
God-filled love.

Does that pin too much hope on the birth of new life? Does it
mean burdening children with unduly great expectations?

For me, there are three reasons why children are incarnate
hopes for a fulfilled life, and are also God's true promises:

1. Every child that is born and accepted represents a new
   beginning of life, a beginning which we do not immediately

comprehend because it is original, unique and incomparable. It is true that we always ask whom this or that child resembles – 'he's the image of his mother', 'she's the image of her father' – because we try to understand what is new and unique only by comparing it with what we already know. We are not prepared for the unique and the new. But at the very moment when we draw on comparisons in this way, and remember what is already familiar, we come upon what is special in a child – original, completely incomparable. This has to be recognized and then respected. But we can only do so if we love the child's own life and keep its future open, so that it can come to itself – not just to us. We must be alive to the magic of the new beginning and must not destroy it through our own plans. We know a child in its unique character only to the extent to which we love it.

2. With every new beginning of life the hope for the fullness of the life we call eternal acquires a new chance and a new assurance. Every child is also a new occasion for hope for the home of life in this unredeemed world. If this were not so we could expect nothing new of beginnings. But 'his mercies are new every morning', we are told (Lam. 3.23). The small and daily renewals of time point beyond themselves to the morning of the new creation of all things. 'And it was evening and it was morning: a new day.' This is also true of a child's birth. Every birth strengthens and confirms the great hope for the victory of life.

3. In my view, the final reason for seeing the beginning of a child's life as the beginning of something new is if we see children not only as the incarnation of our hope for life, but also perceive in them embodiments of God's hopes for us. This is what we are doing when we sense that we are wanted, we are desired and we are expected by God. Human beings are God's great love. Human beings are his dream for his earthly world. Human beings are his image for the earth he loves. God created everything in finished form, but he created human beings in hope. This divine hope that the human beings he created will turn out well can be disappointed, it can miscarry, and it can be disgraced, but the hope cannot be destroyed by human beings. Only God himself can 'repent' –

be sorry – for having created these ambiguous, contradictory men and women. The story of the Flood tells about a 'repentance' like this and about God's profound 'grief' (Gen. 6.6), a grief which only his faithfulness can set aside – his faithful adherence to his will for creation. God's hope for the truly human human being remains steadfast in spite of all the inhumanities which people practise towards each other, towards other creatures and towards the earth. In every child God waits for the human human being. This expectation on God's part must be the deeper reason why 'we are not yet wholly cut off' (Lam. 3.22), and why one generation after another is born. God isn't silent. God isn't dead. God is waiting for the truly human human being. 'In all the prophets I have expected you', Martin Buber makes the Eternal One say to the Messiah, 'and now you have come'. It is from this expectation of God's that we live, and it is into the open time of this divine hope that children are born.

II

Does the Future Belong to the Young?

Chronologically speaking, when we are young life is still ahead of us, while in old age there is not much to lose any more. As time goes on we become old, the future contracts, the past expands. But does this mean that future is a privilege of the young? Do we no longer have any future once we are old? If we look at the future from the standpoint of ageing life, this would seem to be the case. But by future we don't just mean the years ahead; we always mean as well the plenitude of possibilities which challenge our creativity. Otherwise the word 'youth' would have no attraction. So what picture emerges if we look at age from the angle of the future in this sense? However young or old we may be, don't we in every present moment stand at the temporal interface with this future, and don't the future possibilities which we perceive, and in expectation and hope already realize, make us young in a qualitative sense, however old we may be in terms of years? In time we become old, that is true. But in confrontation with the future we can become young if we accept the future's challenges.

But before we look at this reversal in our vision of the future, let us ask about the future chances of the young. Does modern society allow young people their own chances, or does it merely try to dominate them? As examples, we shall look at the way society and the state dealt with three generations of the young in twentieth-century Germany. We shall consider the *Wandervogel* (or 'birds of passage') movement, the Hitler youth, and then the 'consumer' children that followed. These are not mere recollections of the historical past. They are remembrances of the past future.[1]

The Modern Discovery of Youth

In traditional societies of the kind we still find in Africa and Asia today the whole of individual life from the cradle to the grave is laid down in advance, and is ruled by traditional laws and customs. The past dominates the future through the ancestor cult, so every new generation is slotted into the tradition of the elders. The affiliation to families, castes, races and peoples determines the individual's life. There is little scope for personal decision. Consequently a person's first name counts for very little, the family name being all important. The individual consciousness is embedded in the collective consciousness. Because every individual participates in the age-old traditions of the community, and leads his or her life within them, the individual's death too is not experienced as an end; it is seen as a transition to the always present and dominant realm of that person's ancestors. To set a value on the young above that of the old is quite unthinkable in traditional societies.

Societies become 'modern' once they break the dominance of ancestors over those living at the present day, and turn to the young. It is now no longer the past which dominates the spirit of the present and lends bearings to the living; it is the future. Societies also become 'modern' when they begin to set the values of personal liberty above the values of affiliation to traditions. In the wake of the individualization of men and women in the modern world, traditions lose their power to mould the individual and the way people cope with the future. When individuals are set free to determine their own lives, a society becomes creative. A society is called modern when the future begins to fascinate those living in the present as being the open vista of possibilities. Whenever that happens, the living begin to push out the dead. Ancestors are seen simply as 'dead', and are therefore considered to have no more influence. In traditional societies, to be young is the equivalent of being immature and inexperienced. Age takes precedence. The older people sit in the council of the elders and decide about all the important things in society. In modern societies 'young' means the same thing as 'new'. To be young means to be dynamic and capable of a future. Anyone beyond retiring age is viewed as already senile. Innovations in civilization originate with the young, who have courage for the new.

Ever since the beginning of modern times we find the growing value attached to childhood and youth in society, but we also find one cultural revolution after another levelled by the young against society. In 1900 Ellen Kay proclaimed 'the century of the child'. Today, becoming counts for more than being, and children's closeness to nature counts as being more primal than the cultural maturity of the old. First comes the playful liberty of the child, then the 'real' life of adults. The modern faith in progress and a better future for humanity is accompanied by the dream of a youth prepared for the future. In Germany the path of this juvenile culture led first from the free youth movement to the surrender of the young to state control under dictatorship, and later to the commercialization of juvenile culture we have today. Before 1914 my father was an enthusiastic 'free German' *Wandervogel*. In 1939 I became a bored member of the Hitler Youth. Today my grandchildren are computer freaks. These are generations of young people in difficult times.

The German '*Wandervogel*' Youth Movement

The *Wandervogel*, the German youth movement which was formed at the beginning of the twentieth century, was a protest movement against late bourgeois, or middle-class, culture, and the Wilhelminian era (the reign of William II).[2] 'German youth is standing at a historical turning point. Hitherto the young have been excluded from the nation's public life and assigned a passive learning role. They have been reduced to a trivial social life of play, and made mere hangers-on of the older generation. Now youth is beginning to come to itself.' That was the self-confident call of the Free German Youth Movement (the *Freideutsche Jugend*), in its invitation to a famous meeting on the Hoher Meissner (a mountain near Kassel) on 11 and 12 October 1913. In 1900 the young people's association which called itself the *Wandervogel* movement (the 'birds of passage') was founded in Berlin-Steglitz. Together with the young, teachers, doctors and writers streamed 'away from the grey city walls out into the wide world', as their song proclaimed. They looked for a life 'back to nature', roving far afield in search of 'the blue flower' – the image used by the Romantic poets for their cloudy and undefined longings. Stiff collars were exchanged for open-necked shirts, knee breeches took the place of long trousers, loose linen dresses replaced corsets, and evenings in the pub gave way to the campfire, where romantic songs were sung to guitar accompaniment. (These songs were later published under the title the *Zupfgeigenhansel.*) The closely regulated life of middle-class society was replaced by a wild, free, self-determined life in the world of nature.

The *Wandervogel* movement spread rapidly, and by 1914 had about 40,000 members. Everywhere the movement awakened new impulses for a reformed lifestyle, from bioproducts to new styles of dress (or nudism), from art nouveau to fraternities based on early Christian communities (Gottfried Arnold's in the Rhön was an example), or autonomous communes. This youth movement reached its climax with the already mentioned meeting on the Hoher Meissner. Politically it was a deliberate counter-demonstration to the military parade held at the monumental Leipzig memorial on the centenary of the battle of 1813 (the battle of Leipzig) in which Napoleon was defeated. Yet there was no political concept behind this 'First Free German Youth Meeting'. It was rather an idealistic, non-political flight from despised adult society. A protean mix of highly different groups came together, and these groups were able to agree only on what is known as the Meissner formula:

> Free German Youth desires to structure its life on its own terms, on its own responsibility, and with inner sincerity. It will stand up for this inner liberty under all circumstances.

It was also agreed that tobacco and alcohol should be banned from all meetings.

The *Wandervogel* movement was a youthful rebellion. These were the hippies of the Kaiser era, or the flower children of the years of expanding industrialization which followed the establishment of the German empire in 1871. They wanted 'inner liberty' from the conventions of the adult world which weighed them down. Their dreams and utopias remained vague notions about an unscathed world, a life 'back to nature', warm-hearted 'fellowship' instead of the social frigidity of 'society', and 'an association in which the free development of each is the condition for the free development of all', as the Communist Manifesto of 1847 put it. In the *Wandervogel* movement this was called the 'covenant', in which the like-minded pledged themselves to each other. The periodical which Gustav Wynecken published in 1913 was called *Der Anfang* – the beginning. Unfortunately this pre-First World War youth movement was unable to free itself from neo-German nationalism, to which it contributed racist emotions in addition, and it was open to anti-semitism. The movement was as male-dominated as the German empire under William II, and whether girls should be admitted was a topic for prolonged discussion.

The desire for free self-determination was then also soon watered down by well-meaning adult youth workers, who saw to the building of youth hostels and overnight accommodation for hikers. Churches and trade unions, political parties and professional associations all threw themselves into the attempt to 'meet the needs' of youth, or what they believed these to be. They founded their own youth organizations, among others the German Colonial Youth Association (*Deutsche Kolonialjugend*). They did away with the party-political and denominational neutrality which had been the youth movement's original aim, and turned the protest movement of the young into young people's organizations tied to the old traditions and affiliated to their power positions at the time. Today's Young Liberals, Young Socialists, and so on show no more signs of their origin in the protest movement than do the Protestant or Catholic youth organizations, or the young trade unionists, or the young academics. Youth, which had yearned to be the subject of free self-determination, was now reforged into an object whose purpose was to secure the future of the powerful in society.

But the worst thing that burst upon the German youth movement was the storm of patriotic enthusiasm with which, in 1914, the European nations plunged into the First World War. In Langemark, in Flanders, voluntary German student regiments were mowed down by English machine guns – it was said with the German national anthem on their lips. This tragedy became the nationalist myth of the German youth movement, but was in fact its end, and the beginning of the nationalization which overtook it in 1933, with the German dictatorship.

The Hitler Youth

Modern dictatorships in Russia, Italy, Germany and Spain began with the formation of state parties for the control of all the different sectors of public life. All these dictatorships created their state youth movements, for their idea was that 'whoever possesses the young possesses the future'. They took children and young people away from their families, and nationalized their education and upbringing. Anyone who wanted to get on in totalitarian states had to belong to the state's youth movement, through which these governments attempted to extend their present domination into the future. They destroyed every chance for an innovative future because any alternative future was something they wanted to rule out.

After 1933, the Hitler dictatorship in Germany began to take over all the existing youth organizations, the Christian ones as well. The ten- to fourteen-year-olds were organized into the dictatorship's German Youth (*Deutsches Jungvolk*) and Young Girls (*Jungmädel*), the fourteen to eighteen-year-olds into the Hitler Youth (*Hitler Jugend*) or the League of German Girls (*Bund Deutscher Mädchen*).[3] After these came the party organizations – the Nazi party (NSDAP), the SA and the SS. There was a Reich's Youth Leadership, in which not-so-young leaders such as Baldur von Schirach proclaimed that 'the young want to be led by the young'. Boys and girls were isolated from their families so that they might serve the great 'national community'. The elite were educated in special schools, where they were trained for leadership in the Greater Germany that was to come. By way of the state ideology, young people were served up the models and heroes whom they were supposed to imitate. The SS slogan was 'My honour is loyalty', and with that slogan middle-class self-respect and a Christian conscience were driven out of the young people. 'Loyalty is the very marrow of honour.' With these and similar slogans, evoked in countless songs and flag ceremonies, young people were robbed of the will to resist and prepared for unconditional obedience: 'Führer command – we'll follow!' The romanticism of the early youth movement, with its tramps through the countryside, its camps, its nightly campfires, and so forth, still fascinated many young people. They failed to notice that in this guise a pre-military training was already beginning.

In order to unite the people completely, a permanent state of war was proclaimed, war against 'Bolshevism', against 'the Jewish plot to rule the world', against 'plutocracy', and whatever enemy was allegedly at hand. The whole of life took the imprint of friend-enemy thinking. 'He who is not for us is against us' and must be exterminated.

The slogans of political messianism, such as 'we are the future', and 'with us the new era is coming', trained young people to self-dedication and prepared them for self-sacrifice. The capacity for enthusiasm about their own future was exploited, for this hope gave many of them a sense that they were of value. The Nazi ideology engendered a political youth religion. In Germany these generations of young people were sacrificed as victims in the Second World War. They died in Stalingrad and Kursk. They did not only die in a war that was hopeless from the beginning. They also died for the appalling crimes against humanity committed by their leaders and the men in power.

The nationalization of young people we experienced in the dictatorships of the twentieth century dispossessed children of their childhood and destroyed their youth. The youth cult of modern dictators did not open up a future for the young. It destroyed that future. Because dictators permit no innovative future, they deny the whole of society its chance for renewal.

Consumer Children

Children and young people are by no means always viewed as the hope of a modern society. Since they are also society's weakest members, they are exposed without any defence to every kind of adult exploitation and violence. Children have no lobby we say, although politically nearly all countries have ratified the UN

Convention on Children's Rights.[4] In the countries with a free market economy we can observe the increasingly aggressive commercialization of childhood and youth[5] which followed the discovery that the child was an economic resource and that children have potential purchasing power of over 10 billion dollars per year. Children turn into customers. Child-geared advertising reaches into the nursery, the school, the sports club and the football stadium, until children find it cool and trendy and ace to appear in the latest fashion. As the jeans ads show, youth advertising doesn't confine itself to what can be bought; it simultaneously passes on the equivalent youth culture. For some time, in Germany too, advertising experts have been active in state schools (schools, that is, which children are bound to attend, unless their parents opt for, and can afford, the private sector). The reward is school sponsoring by the firms concerned, which provide computers and laptops as new teaching aids. Teenage magazines, branded articles and Coca Cola ads are supposed to look down enticingly from the classroom walls, so as to accustom the children to real life. School marketing firms make their way into school books too. Whether one pillories this as consumer terror or lauds it as a part of modern life, as long as there is compulsory schooling, advertising in schools means robbing school children of their freedom. This must be prevented through a government prohibition of advertising in state schools.

In the United States classroom advertising is evidently widespread. Without money from industry some schools could not survive. So they sign contracts with sponsors, and permit the advertising. The Center for Commercial-free Public Education complains that 'the commercialization of America's classrooms has taken on epidemic proportions'. But fast-food chains, soft-drink producers and sportswear manufacturers fight for the attention of the teenagers and for the goodwill of the teachers. Coca Cola and Pepsi wage advertising battles in school playgrounds. The state of California has meanwhile forbidden commercial logos in school books, but 'the sell-out of America's children' continues.

The success is ambiguous. On the one hand young people are trained early on to be consumers, and are made dependent on particular products; but on the other hand they soon already become immune to advertising. If one sees too many commercials one ceases to take them in, and can't remember any of them when one is shopping.

To structure one's own life in free self-determination was the ideal of the German youth movement. It is what every individual is destined for. But not everyone has the personal strength to fulfil this destiny, and many people lack the external opportunities to do so. So the important thing for parents, teachers and the public generally is to build up the necessary strength among children and young people, and to make them capable of seizing their chances in life. The essential preconditions for this are respect for the future of the young themselves, and curiosity about their own decisions. To withdraw and let children come to themselves is a way of opening up for them the living space they need.

The Future Makes Us Young

Finally, we come back to our initial question: does the future belong to the young, or does the future make us young? With every child a new life begins, and when we are young we see many years stretching ahead of us. But does this mean that as the years go by, the future is slowly but inexorably lost to us? By no means. There are times, as we have seen, when the state and society give children and young people no chance. There are also children who refuse to live, and who are afraid of failure. There are young people who despise the world, and who are a prey to resignation; and there is always the temptation to 'opt out'. Nor is it true that the young are particularly progressive by nature, and that we become more conservative as we grow old. Future as the quintessence of life's possibilities and the challenge to a new beginning is confined neither to childhood nor youth. No one is too old to begin something new, even if we can never begin the same thing a second time. So are the young especially creative by nature simply by virtue of their youth? Creative powers are awakened at every age, when new possibilities emerge and if they are recognized as such. In this sense we are always standing at the beginning.

On 18 August 2002 the 82-year-old pope John Paul II, ill as he was, was warmly greeted in his home town Cracow by a huge crowd. 'You are young', they cried again and again to the frail old man, 'You are young!' He smiled appreciatively but answered in a quavering voice. 'No, that isn't true.' As far as his prospects of living are concerned, he was of course right. But as far as his spirit and his influence goes, it was the people who saw him as young who were the discerning ones. The prophet Isaiah already saw things in just this way:

> Youths shall faint and be weary, and young men shall fall exhausted;
> But they who wait for the Lord shall renew their strength,
> They shall mount up with wings like eagles,
> They shall run and not be weary,
> They shall walk and not faint.

(Isa. 40. 30–31)

PART TWO

IN MY END
IS MY BEGINNING

⇢⇠

There is saying that every beginning is hard. But beginnings are particularly hard if we have to start all over again a second time, or are forced to undertake something completely new. Then the beginning may have been preceded by a painful end, or by one that has left a heavy weight. There are the catastrophes in which we have lost everything dear to us. Or there are the evils which wickedness disseminates, which destroy life – on the one side the sufferings and humiliations, and on the other side the guilt. How can we begin if in one way or other we have come to the end? Where are the energies which can free us from the burdens of the past and give us new courage for the future? Where do new vistas open up? No one is perfect. Few people achieve a life without caesuras or disruption. There are hardly any lives which are completely rounded off early on, or where people feel that they have had their fill of life. Limitations, disruptions, thwartings and impediments play a part in most of our own biographies. But how do we cope with them? How do we get up again after we have fallen – or when catastrophes we could do nothing about have fallen on us?

In the second part of this little doctrine of hope I shall first go into a history of catastrophes and new beginnings: for biblical theology is a *catastrophe theology,* from the story of the Flood to the apocalyptic terrors of the end-time announced in the book of Revelation. In the second section I shall put forward the justice and righteousness of God, and the rebirth of life, in the context of the evil which causes suffering on the one hand and on the other guilt. I shall look critically at the traditional Lutheran and Catholic teachings about the justification of the sinner, and shall expand them to take in the establishment of justice for the victims of evil. Justifying faith is the courage for a new beginning, and a rebirth to a living hope. In the final section I shall try to arrive at a spirituality of the attentive life. I shall conclude this central part of the book with a meditation on the vital energy of hope and the deadly power of despair.

III

New Beginnings in Catastrophes: Biblical Catastrophe Theology

Personal Experiences

I shall begin with some personal reminiscences. This doesn't fit into the conventional template of what is expected of a professor in a German university, but for the subject we are considering it is necessary. For I am not only a theologian who is concerned with the hopes and fears of humanity on the scholarly level. I am also a survivor of 'Sodom and Gomorrah'. To say this is not poetic licence in the religious sense. It is painful fact. Whenever I call up that catastrophe and descend into the dark pit of remembrance, I am overwhelmed again by fear and trembling. I am talking here about the destruction of my home city of Hamburg in the last week of July 1943. Night after night, about a thousand Royal Air Force bombers appeared over the city, and with explosive and incendiary bombs kindled a storm of fire which in east Hamburg, from Hammerbrook to Wandsbek, burnt everything living and reduced every home to rubble. During those nights and in that fire 40,000 people died. Ironically, the code name given to this destruction by the RAF was Operation Gomorrah. Together with others belonging to my school class, I was an air force auxiliary in an anti-aircraft battery in the inner city. The battery was stationed on the Outer Alster, easily visible for aircraft, and it was completely wiped out in a hailstorm of bombs. But for some incomprehensible reason, the bomb which blew to pieces the school friend who stood beside me at the firing platform left me unscathed. I found myself in the water, clinging to a plank of wood, and was saved.

Things had begun when radar reported huge swarms of
bombers approaching over the North Sea. When the bombers
were over us, they dropped strips of aluminium foil, which
blinded and jammed the radar devices. No more counter-action
was possible, and no defence. In the end, those of us who had
survived made our way through the wreckage of the streets,
climbing over charred bodies. We were convinced that this was
indeed 'the end', and that the war would be over in a few days.
But this terrible end was followed by two other years of unending
terror which destroyed the lives of millions. There is no need to
describe it any further. But for the description of Hamburg as
Sodom and Gomorrah I should only like to add that during the
Nazi dictatorship about 40,000 people were murdered in the
Neuengamme concentration camp near the city, and about
50,000 Hamburg Jews in White Russia. That too is part of the
catastrophe which I escaped. At that time I was 17 years old.
What effect did this catastrophe have on me?

I come from a secular Hamburg family of teachers. My grand-
father was Grand Master of a Freemasons' Lodge in Hamburg,
and had left the Church. For me, religion and theology were
totally remote. I wanted to study mathematics and physics. Max
Planck and Albert Einstein were the secret heroes of my youth.
Goethe's poems and Nietzsche's *Zarathustra* gave form to my
feelings and the stirrings of my awakening mind. But in that
catastrophic night, for the first time in my life I cried out to God:
'God, where are you?' That was my question in the face of death.
It was not the theodicy question we are all familiar with – the
question, how can God allow this to happen? That always seems
to me like an onlooker's question. The person who is in the grip
of a catastrophe, or is already in the jaws of a mass death, asks
differently about God. And then came the other question, the
one which has haunted me all my life ever since: why am I still
alive and not dead like the rest?

Three years as a prisoner of war, from 1945 to 1948, gave me
time enough to search for answers to these two questions. In the
first year particularly it was for me a struggle with the question
about God. Like Jacob, wrestling at the brook Jabbok with a
dark and mysterious angel, I tormented myself with God's dark
and mysterious side, with his hidden face and his deadly 'no'

which had put me in misery behind barbed wire. At the end of 1945 a well-meaning army chaplain gave me a Bible. I must have looked at him somewhat uncomprehendingly: a Bible of all things! I then went on to read it without much understanding until I came to Israel's psalms of lament. Psalm 39 caught my attention: 'I am dumb and must eat up my suffering within myself' (Luther's rendering) '. . . My life is as nothing before you . . . I am a stranger as all my fathers were.' Those were words that echoed what was in my own heart, now that Goethe and Nietzsche no longer had anything to say to me. Later I read Mark's Gospel. And when I came to Jesus' death cry: 'My God, why have you forsaken me?' I was profoundly struck. I knew: this is the one who understands you. I began to understand the Christ who was assailed by God and suffered from God, because I felt that he understood me. That gave me new courage to live. I saw colours again, heard music again, and felt the stirrings of renewed vitality.

The kindness which Scottish miners and English neighbours showed the German prisoners of war who were at that time their enemies shamed us profoundly. We were accepted as people, even though we were only numbers and wore the prisoner's patch on our backs. But that made it possible for us to live with the guilt of our own people, the catastrophes we had brought about and the long shadows of Auschwitz, without repressing them and without becoming callous.

In that Scottish camp I arrived at Christian faith and decided to study theology. Mathematical problems lost their charm. True, I had no idea what the Church was about, but I was looking for an assurance that would sustain existence, and asked about the truth of the Christian faith. In 1948 I returned to Hamburg, limping indeed like Jacob but 'blessed'. That was my new beginning, the beginning I arrived at when Hamburg was at its end: in the end was my beginning.

Two experiences set a permanent mark on me.

First, I discovered that in every end a new beginning lies hidden. It will find you if you look for it. Don't lose heart!

Second, I found that if one gathers the courage to live again, the chains begin to smart, but the pain is better than the dull resignation in which nothing matters, and one is more dead than alive.

The Flood and the Covenant with Noah: An Archetypal Image of the End of the World

The remembrance that the earth had once been destroyed by a great flood finds a place in the sagas of many peoples and in their myths about the world's beginnings. For mainland dwellers, floods were always a symbol of the chaos that ruled before the world was created. 'The earth was without form and void ... and the Spirit of God hovered over the waters', begins the account of creation in the Bible. So the ordered creation of a world which brings forth life and sustains it is a world we have to treat justly and with care. The story of Noah and the Flood belongs to the genre 'saga'. Sagas tell of something in prehistory which no one can have observed. In sagas like this the truth is veiled. But the people concerned recognize it, and we can uncover it with a little detective expertise. The saga of the Flood can be found in the book of Genesis, chapters 6 to 9. I shall recall the story briefly, bringing out the points which were taken up later in the apocalyptic writings about a final downfall of the world still to come.

Why the great and all-destroying Flood?

The reason given for the great Flood which destroyed all life on earth is human 'wickedness', and the resulting corruption of all earthly living things. 'And God said to Noah: I have determined to make an end of all flesh [i.e. life]; for the earth is filled with wickedness through them; behold I will destroy them with the earth' (6.13). 'All flesh had spoilt its path on earth' is Luther's rendering. The 'wickedness' the passage talks about is not a matter of individual sins. It is a 'corruption' which has spread over the whole earth as the sphere of living things. Here human beings are seen in the context of the whole biosphere; they are not set over against it, as they are today in the anthropomorphism of the modern world. It is not only the biosphere that is affected. It is even the earth itself, as the living space for everything that exists on it and lives from it: 'God saw the earth, and behold, it was corrupt' (Gen. 6.12). The Hebrew words for this comprehensive corruption are never used as terms for sin. They mean something special and unique, an extremity of wickedness. So what is this wickedness which has laid hold of all life on earth? 'The violent acts of humanity had taken on such proportions that they had corrupted, destroyed the earth, the human world. The earth as it should be, with the purpose for which God created it, was destroyed . . . [This "wickedness"] is not used in a general sense, meaning sin or wrong . . . it is used in the original sense of violence, crime, which consists in bloodshed, criminal oppression and force.'[1] This is what the earth is full of. That is to say, it has already been destroyed as far as its life-bringing functions are concerned (Gen. 1.24). That is the catastrophe brought upon life by human beings, and it is the precursor of the natural catastrophe of the Flood.

How did this deadly wickedness come about?

The text as we now have it is made up of several different parts, which have been welded into a single story.

In verse 5 'The Lord saw that the wickedness of man was great in the earth and that every imagination of the thoughts of his heart was only evil continually.' That sounds like Augustine's doctrine of original sin. But verse 4 gives a particular reason: 'There were tyrants on earth in those days when the sons of God came in to the daughters of men, and they bore children to them. These became violent men in the world, and men of renown.' This saga has initially nothing to do with the story of the Flood. Who are these primordial 'sons of God' who copulate with human 'daughters' and beget heroes? Ever since the book of Enoch, metaphysical hybrid unions of this kind have been called by some people 'angel marriages', as with the angels in Wim Bender's renowned German film *Himmel über Berlin*. Others suppose that this was a group of lower gods, who fell upon human women: Titans, giants, monstrous figures belonging to the primordial past. But if we read the story retrospectively, we get another picture. In the political world of antiquity, who was it that called himself 'Son of God', 'Son of Heaven'? Who were the people who traced their ancestry back not to human beings but to the gods? It was the godlike pharaohs in Egypt, the Assyrian rulers, the Chinese and Persian emperors who let themselves be worshipped as gods and behaved as 'tyrants'. It is from these that the violence proceeds which brings ruin on the whole earth. They are not filled with 'spirit'; they are 'flesh', as verse 3 puts it. That is to say, they have no desire to protect life, but have made a covenant with death. Their rule of violence rests on an arbitrary threat of death, used to oppress the nations, and on a ruthless exploitation of the fertile regions of the earth, for the purpose of feeding their own capital cities and their armies. It is these who are the source of organized violence against life. The wickedness leading to the catastrophe which overtakes all life on earth is to be found in the organized crimes of the despotisms and tyrannies which extort obedience through death, subjugate peoples through genocide, enrich themselves at the expense of nature, and leave behind them a ravaged earth. In systems of rule like this, it is death that reigns, not life. The modern expression for this is structural sin. What is meant are the unjust structures in political and economic life which despoil life and disseminate death.

This interpretation of the story of the Flood is not new. In Roman times the Christian martyrs refused to conform to the emperor cult because they believed that these rulers together with their gods were the offspring of the fornication between angels and 'the daughters of men' they had raped; they belonged to 'the demon brood' of 'tyrants, violent men and men of renown' about whom Gen. 6.4 speaks.[2]

How does the Creator react to this perversion of his earthly creatures?

The nature of God's reaction is important for later apocalyptic thinking and its catastrophe theology. 'The Lord saw that the wickedness of human beings was great . . . and he was sorry (AV: repented) that he had made human beings on the earth' (6.5f.). 'So he said: I will blot out the human beings whom I have created from the face of the ground, man and beast and creeping things and birds of the air, for I am sorry that I have made them' (6.7).

The creation of human beings, and then their threatened annihilation: the contradiction is drawn from experience. But in this story it is not interpreted as a struggle between different gods, and not even as a struggle of the One God against evil. It is seen as being a conflict in God himself: God 'was sorry' for having created human beings and 'it grieved him to his heart' (6.6b). As God sees creation now, it is by no means 'very good' (which was the way he initially saw it according to the end of the first creation account, Gen. 1.31). On the contrary: it is very bad. We might say that God's creation had gone wrong. God suffers from the corruption of what he has created. This grief has rightly been called 'the divine pain'.[3] In order to surmount it, the Creator revokes his resolve to create, and lets his earthly creation perish. That is God's 'repentance' – his act of regret. Because what he has created has gone astray, the Creator takes the responsibility for its corruption on himself. He 'repents' – he is sorry – and destroys what he has apparently made wrongly.

A Jewish interpretation asks: why did God create men and women at all, since he must after all have known that they would cause him grief? The story of the Flood supplies the answer: God had made a mistake, and he goes back on his creation of human beings. I don't believe, as some have thought,[4] that God's pain is pain over the punishment he has to impose on the corrupt world, for he is not bound to impose it. It is his pain over the unsuccessful outcome of his creation which leads him to revoke his creative resolve. As long as God punishes the wickedness of human beings he is concerned about them and believes in their possible betterment. But here he quits the creation of human beings, and turns away from them. That God could finally let his creation drop, as futile and corrupt – that he might turn away from the earth and allow it to sink into chaos: this was always the ultimate anxiety in all the Jewish and Christian apocalypses. For that would be not merely a catastrophe for the world; it would be a catastrophe in God too, his total eclipse, the self-destruction of this world's Creator. 'He was sorry that he had made human beings.' That brief sentence encapsulates the most terrible theology we can conceive of.

In the end the new beginning

That is the way we might describe the saving of Noah, his family, and all the many beasts in his ark. The annihilation of the humanity that had gone wrong and the rescue of the one human being belong together. Once again, the single person is not delivered just by himself; he is saved together with the animal species for a new world of living things. Human beings and all the living on earth still belong together in a single biosphere. It is said of humanity-gone-wrong that it had been corrupted by its violence, and had ruined all life on earth. It is said of the one person: 'I have seen that you are righteous before me in this generation' (Gen. 7.1). Noah, the one righteous person in a race corrupted by violence! He alone is told about the coming catastrophe, so that he can build the ark that will provide safety. He is told the exact time of the catastrophe, so that he can go into the ark with his family and all the animal species before the great rain begins. The rest of the human race is overtaken by the catastrophe, as if by a merciless fate. We are not told about any reactions on the part of the people concerned: 'No lament, cry, death agony – nothing at all of this sort. The effect of the great Flood is absolute silence.'[5] The people are not even told of the impending judgement.

We all know the rest of the story. After the Flood has destroyed everything on earth (7.23) a wind gets up and the water-level falls. Noah and his ark land, allegedly on Mount Ararat, which was later for all apocalyptists to become 'the place of safety at the end of the world'. Then God makes a new covenant with Noah, his descendants and all living things (9.9f.). He reiterates the command given at creation: 'Be fruitful and multiply, and fill the earth' (Gen. 9.1). The vegetarianism of paradise is now supplemented by animal food (but without the blood). Fratricide is to be punished by death. In other words, the acts of violence against man and beast which are always humanly possible are fenced round by divine commandments. But the Creator for his part promises 'never again to curse the ground' (8.21), and that 'never again shall there be a flood to destroy the earth' (9.11). As a sign of his faithfulness the rainbow will appear in the dark clouds which could bring the great rain (9.13f.).

But what does that mean for the conflict, the dissonance, in God himself? Apparently in God's heart faithfulness to his resolve to create conquers his regret at having created these wicked and violent human beings. God remains faithful to his creation, even when the beings he has created do everything to ruin themselves and their world. This means that for God a time of patience begins. God endures this human world without destroying it. He leaves it time to live and gives it living space, and in this way he preserves the created world in spite of its self-contradictions. The primal, the ur-catastrophe has come to a stop. Everything that still exists afterwards is grace. To put it more precisely: everything that comes and endures after the catastrophe and is not again destroyed issues from God's pain over the beings he has created, who are ruining themselves. God suffers the world in its contradictions, and endures it in his long-suffering, instead of annihilating it. He takes on himself the dissonance between the world's creation and its corruption, so that in spite of its corruption the world may live.

Israel's Catastrophe and the Beginning of Judaism

In 587 BCE the Assyrians under Nebuchadnezzar destroyed Jerusalem and the Temple. That was the end of the kingdom of Judah as an independent state, and for a large section of the population it was the beginning of 70 years of Babylonian captivity. The prophecies of Israel's God about 'the promised land' and the 'great people' had been fulfilled. These promises were now shattered. Yet in exile Judaism was born. Solomon's Temple was destroyed by Israel's enemies. But what began was the gathering of the Scriptures, the Torah and the Prophets. The political Temple religion gave way to the scriptural religion. The religion of a tiny Middle Eastern people became a universal religion of exile. Out of the catastrophe of Israel as a political entity, Jewish messianism was born. This transformation process seems to be unique in the history of religion. Let us look at the political catastrophe and the way it was theologically mastered. *Churban*, destruction, is the name given to this first catastrophe of Israel's; later to the destruction of Jerusalem by the Romans in 70 CE; and finally to Auschwitz.

The destruction of Jerusalem is described by Israelite historiographers in 2 Kings, chapters 24 and 25, in order that it may be a perpetual remembrance. In the conflict between the Great Powers, the last king in Judah, Zedekiah, had pinned his hopes to Egypt, not to Assyria. 'But the king of Egypt did not come again out of his land' (24.7). So the little country on the tongue of land between the major powers was left to the mercy of Assyria. Nebuchadnezzar came 'with all his army' and besieged Jerusalem 'and built siege works against it round about'. Finally, after famine had broken out in the city, Jerusalem was stormed. King Zedekiah fled, but was captured and brought before the king of Babylon. Nebuchadnezzar had Zedekiah's children slain in front of their father, and then put out his eyes, after which he was taken away in chains as prisoner. In Jerusalem the palaces and Solomon's Temple were burnt. The city walls were torn down, all the treasures were stolen, and people were carried off into captivity in Babylon. Only a few peasants and vine-growers were left behind. Judah became an Assyrian province. That was the end of Israel, for the Northern kingdom had been destroyed previously.[6]

It was not just the end of Israel politically. It was its end religiously too; for everything which Israel had seized possession of in the land of Canaan was viewed by the people as the fulfilment of the promises of its God, at whose command the people had left their Egyptian captivity. The exodus from slavery, God's covenant on Sinai with the liberated people, and the entry into 'the promised land' of liberty were the elements constituting Israel's faith in God and at the same time its whole existence. Trust in the protection of this God, whose house stood in the centre of Jerusalem, was shattered once the Temple was destroyed. In confrontation with the powerful gods of Assyria, Israel's God had proved himself to be a powerless idol, and by surrendering his people and his Temple he had also broken his covenant with that people. It would have been no more than logical if the conquered people had gone over to the mightier gods of the victors, as was otherwise normal practice in the political history of the religions. It would have been no more than consistent if the survivors of this catastrophe had abandoned their existence as God's people. How could one still have any desire to be an Israelite after a catastrophe like this? How can one still bring up children as Jews after Auschwitz? Evidently there was indeed some Jewish assimilation to the new environment in Babylon, with its culture and religion. But what nevertheless kept Israel alive after this catastrophe, and preserved Jewish identity? There were a number of ways in which this was achieved. I shall mention only two of them.

(a) Through its prophets, the people interpreted the catastrophe as the judgement of its God on its own injustice and unrighteousness, its breach of the law, and its idolatry. The God of Israel was not helpless when the Assyrians destroyed the holy city: he had 'hidden his face' (*hester panim*), and delivered his people up to the consequences of its godlessness. Through his judgement, Jerusalem was indeed destroyed, but the God who judged still kept his covenant with his chosen people and did not abandon them. So it was possible to appeal to him for help and for a renewed deliverance from captivity.

But where was God? How did the people conceive of his presence in the foreign country? 'I will be your God and you shall be my people': that was God's covenant with this people. But the covenant embraces another promise too: 'I will dwell in the midst of the Israelites.'[7] This dwelling of God's in the midst of his people was made visible through the Ark of the Covenant, which the people of God took with them on their wanderings, as a portable altar. David conquered Jerusalem and brought the Ark into the city. Solomon built the Temple, and from then on God 'dwelt' there, in the Temple's Holy of Holies. But what happened to this indwelling of God's (the Shekinah as it was called) when the Temple went up in flames? Did the Shekinah return to God in heaven? That would have been the end for Israel as God's people. Or did the the Shekinah continue to dwell 'in the midst of the Israelites', moving with the people into Babylonian captivity? Then the people can be God's people even in exile and among foreign peoples, and can experience his presence in suffering. Through his Shekinah the eternal, infinite God became the companion on the way and the fellow-sufferer, the one who is persecuted with his dispersed people and suffers with them. 'Where two or three bend over the Torah, there am I in the midst of them', says a rabbinic saying, talking about God's Shekinah. This self-humiliation on God's part and his self-surrender to the fate of his people can be termed the new theological perception of God which followed Israel's catastrophe. Religiously speaking, it kept alive the people expelled from their homeland and driven into forced labour in Babylon.

(b) We find the second great response to the catastrophe that had been suffered in the visions of the exilic prophets about Israel's future. They do not prophesy a totally new future. Instead they pick up from Israel's history the recollections of God's great acts before the catastrophe, and transport these memories into the future of the coming God. The old remembrances, extinguished in the catastrophe, become new messianic hopes.[8]

The prophets announce a new Exodus, the future exodus from the Babylonian captivity. Unlike the first Exodus, which took place secretly by night, this will be like a solemn daytime procession, moving publicly through the desert into the promised land of old (Isa. 40), and at the head of the procession will be God the Lord himself (Isa. 52.12).

Jeremiah prophesies that God will give his people a new covenant, in which the law will not be held up to them on stone tablets; it will be written 'upon their hearts'. Righteousness and justice will be spontaneous. No one will teach other people, for all will know God as he is (Jer. 31.34).

God will build a new Jerusalem, which will be more wonderful than the old Jerusalem ever was.

And from the tribe of David God will 'raise up' the messiah king who will bring justice and righteousness not just to Israel but to the poor and to all the nations as well. His sovereignty will have no end (Isa. 9, 11 and 12).

God will send a new Servant of God like Moses. He will not act through miracles and deeds of power, but will redeem the world through his suffering. 'Through his wounds we are healed' (Isa. 53).

The Golgotha Catastrophe
and the Beginning of Christianity

Christianity also issued from a catastrophe, the catastrophe of the crucifixion on Golgotha of the Messiah Jesus by the Roman occupying power.

If we want to understand this catastrophe rightly, we have to look back to Jesus' beginnings in Galilee. At the very time when John the Baptist, the preacher of repentence, was first imprisoned and then beheaded by Herod, Jesus came forward publicly and, like John, proclaimed: 'The kingdom of God is at hand: repent.' But he saw this closeness of God's kingdom not in judgement, like John, but in grace – in the gospel (Mark 1.15). God is not waiting any longer. God is coming to meet human beings. Jesus doesn't proclaim this in words alone. He shows it by healing the sick and by driving out the tormenting spirits whom the people called 'demons'. Jesus 'forgave sins', the Gospels report, and by doing so he intervened in what was the right of the divine Judge alone. John was an ascetic. He lived in the desert, ate grass-hoppers and wild honey and was dressed only in camel skins (Mark 1.6). But Jesus went into the villages and lived with the people. He was denounced for being a 'glutton and a wine-drinker'. What had he done? Instead of avoiding the impure 'tax-collectors and sinners', he had accepted them and eaten with them in their own houses. Jesus left his family and lived with the simple people, taught them his gospel in the Sermon on the Mount we are familiar with, and called them to discipleship. 'He was sorry for the people.' Jesus no longer addressed the God of Israel obediently as 'Lord', but trustfully, using the intimate word 'Abba', dear Father. I need not elaborate any further: Jesus lived in the presence of God's coming kingdom and acted out of an unheard-of inner bond with God.

We don't know who Jesus believed himself to be. But for his disciples, men and women, for the sick and the despised sinners, and for the poor among the people he was nothing less than the promised messiah-king. That is why when he entered Jerusalem the people cried: 'Blessed is he who comes in the name of the Lord! Blessed is the kingdom of our father David that is coming!' (Mark 11.9f.). The people saw Jesus as the kingdom of God in person, as the promised messiah who would not only heal their sicknesses and purify them from their sins, but would also liberate them from the foreign rule of the Romans. 'We hoped that he was the one to redeem Israel', confessed the disciples on the road to Emmaus (Luke 24.21).

(a) And then came the catastrophe. One of the disciples, Judas, betrays him to the Romans, probably hoping to challenge him to rebellion. But Jesus unresistingly lets himself be taken prisoner. During Pilate's interrogation he certainly acknowledges that he is 'king of the Jews': 'You have said so' (Mark 1.2). But he does none of the things that were to be expected of Israel's royal liberator. That evidently makes the faithful disciple Peter waver. He follows Jesus 'from afar', but when he is recognized 'he denies him three times'. 'I do not know the man', he says, in order to save his own skin (Luke 22.54–62). The other disciples run away, not just out of fear of the Romans but out of embitterment over the helpless master they had followed. The climax of disappointment follows, the disappointment Jesus himself suffers through God himself. The prayer in Gethsemane – 'Let this cup pass from me' – is not heard by God his Father. Jesus dies on the Roman cross in the profoundest God-forsakenness: 'My God, why have you forsaken me?' is said to have been his final word. That was the end of Jesus the Messiah, the end of his message about the nearness of the kingdom of God, the end of the God whom he had addressed so intimately as 'Abba', the end of his divine sonship, the end of every trust that had been placed in him, whoever the trusting person may have been.

(b) Yet his end became his true beginning. His public death was followed by the Easter appearances, to the faithful women at his tomb first of all, and then to the disciples who had fled into Galilee; and with these appearances the new beginning was inaugurated.[9] The disciples proclaimed that the dead Christ had 'appeared' to them as the eternally Living One in the radiant glory of the coming God. The Greek word used for this 'appearing' can mean 'he appeared to them', 'he let himself be seen' or 'he was revealed to them'. But the disciples failed to recognize him. He had first to identify himself through the marks of his wounds, through his voice, or through the breaking of bread.

When they recognized him, he immediately 'vanished out of their sight' (Luke 24.31).

Among the disciples these tremendous and unexampled 'appearances' of the crucified Jesus first evoked incredulous astonishment. It was the Christ who appeared to them who first had to challenge them to 'believe'. Evidently the appearances of Christ radiated powerful spiritual efficacies and new vital energies, through which the disciples were transformed. In order to find a common denominator for the two experiences – the terrible experience of Jesus' helpless, God-forsaken death on the cross and the reviving and quickening experience of his presence in the divine glory – and in order to understand what had happened to him, they took up the ancient Israelite symbol of hope, 'the resurrection of the dead', and talked about Christ's 'resurrection from the dead': he was the One ahead of all others as 'the first fruits of them that sleep' and 'the leader of life', as Paul put it. For the disciples this was not a reanimation of someone who had died, nor was it a ghostly 'return' of the dead. Jesus was not seemingly dead. He had really died and really been buried. Nor was it his spirit that appeared to them; it was Jesus himself in the transfigured form of the resurrection world. Consequently this event was for them not a past event, something in history finished and done with; it was an event in the past which still has its future ahead of it. That is to say, it was what theological language describes as an *eschatological* event, in which God's future has acquired potency over the past.

The disciples who had once fled then returned to Jerusalem and proclaimed publicly the raising of Christ from the dead and the open horizon of his sovereignty. This about-turn from disappointment to certainty and from deadly fear to a faith which is not afraid of death is the real proof of the reality of Christ's resurrection; for in Jerusalem the disciples were bound to expect persecution by the Romans and death, as adherents of the executed 'terrorist' Jesus of Nazareth; while among the Jews they couldn't have stood their ground for a day with their proclamation of Christ's resurrection from the dead if his body had still been lying in the tomb. 'The empty tomb' itself is not a proof of Christ's resurrection, for it could have been empty for a different reason, if the body had been removed by other people. It is the proclamation of the resurrection by the disciples in Jerusalem which is a proof of the empty tomb.

When the crucified hope of the disciples was reawakened, their resurrection faith acted in the ancient world like an explosion of hearts and senses. With elemental force it attacked the ruling powers of this world: the power of evil, the inevitability of death, the hell of God-forsakenness. If the Christ forsaken by God has been raised, then hell is vanquished. If the buried Christ has risen from the dead, then the end of death as our inevitable destiny is in sight. 'Death is swallowed up in the victory of life.' If the one crucified by the Romans has been exalted to be the Lord of God's coming kingdom, then that is the end of the Roman rule of violence. The murderers will not in the final resort triumph over their victims.

The resurrection message burst through frontiers and was universal: Christ has been raised not as an individual but as Israel's messiah, as the Son of man of the nations, as humanity's 'new Adam', and as 'the first born of all creation'. The Orthodox Easter icon brings out the collective character of Christ's resurrection particularly well: the resurrection begins in the world of the dead. The risen Christ pulls Adam with his right hand and Eve with his left, and with them draws the whole of humanity out of the world of death into the transfigured world of eternal life. His new beginning in his end is the beginning of God's new world in the passing away of this one. Whether this world will come to an end, and whatever that end may be, the Christian hope says: God's future has already begun. With Christ's resurrection from the catastrophe of Golgotha the new beginning has already been made, a beginning which will never again pass away because it issues from the victory over transience.

Catastrophes of the Modern World: An End without a Beginning?

Out of their recollections of the catastrophes we have described, Jewish and Christian apocalypses gave form to their fears about a coming downfall of the world. According to the apocryphal Book of Enoch (1.7), 'the earth shall be wholly rent in sunder,

and all that is upon the earth shall perish, and there shall be a
judgment upon all'.[10] But out of their recollections of the new
beginnings after these catastrophes, the apocalyptists developed
images of hope in the perils of the world: 'On that day Mine Elect
One shall sit on the throne of glory . . . Then I will cause Mine
Elect One to dwell among them, and I will transform the heaven
. . . and I will transform the earth' (45. 4). We find very similar
hopes portrayed in the Christian book of Revelation, in chapters
20 and 21. But behind the fears about the world's end is always
the fear about God – the fear that after the new wickedness of
men and women God could again, and this time finally, 'repent'
of having made these creatures who have turned out so badly.
And that is why in the downfall of the world the apocalyptists
search for the face of God.

Today's phrase 'apocalypse now' is distinct from these apocalyptic traditions of hope. It is used as a term for catastrophes of
our own making: the nuclear catastrophe which has suddenly
become possible, and the creeping ecological catastrophe too –
that is to say, crimes against humanity and crimes against nature.
Human beings were to blame for earlier catastrophes, but the
catastrophes themselves were brought about by God the Judge;
here, however, human beings are guilty of actually bringing
about the end itself. Earlier, people expected the end to come
from God, and hoped that from God the new beginning would
come. But today we have to do with self-made apocalypses, for
which human beings have to take responsibility, not God.
Consequently these are End-times without hope. There is no
'nuclear Armageddon in our generation', as President Ronald
Reagan maintained, wishing to push off on to God what he
himself was prepared, if need be, to set off himself by pressing the
decisive button. Modern exterminism with the methods of mass
annihilation therefore does not deserve the name of apocalypse.
The 'exterminator' in the science-fiction horror films has nothing
in common with the Son of man and judge of the biblical apocalypses. The one comes to cut down, the other to raise up.

Today there is a frightening terrorism which is making the
transition from passive expectation of the world's end to its
active ending. This terrorism can take on religious features,
but it can be anarchistic too. In the last century, the Russian

anarchist Michael Bakunin already proclaimed the slogan: 'The lust to destroy is also a creative lust', and with this philosophy justified the murder of the Tsar and the suicide of the murderers. 'Without destruction there can be no reconstruction', was the watchword Mao Tse-Tung gave the youthful cultural revolution in China. It cost the life of millions and reduced supreme cultural monuments to rubble. No 'reconstruction' ever happened. Pol Pot and his Khmer Rouge murdered two million people belonging to the older generation on the killing fields in Cambodia, with the aim of building 'a new world' with the young. What was left behind was a ravaged country. When this terrorism allies itself with apocalyptic ideas, the outcome is often the mass suicide of the sect's adherents: in 1978 in Jonestown, Guyana, 912 members of a popular temple sect; in 1995 in Canada and Switzerland 53 adherents of a Sun Temple sect; in 1997 in San Diego 39 believers belonging to a UFO death-cult sect; in the year 2000 in Uganda over 1,000 people belonging to a Catholic sect devoted to the Virgin Mary. There can also be attempts at a mass murder of unbelievers and the godless, as with the poison-gas sect of Shoko Asahara in Tokyo and the American Oklahoma bomber.

The scenario of the crime committed on 11 September 2001 in the World Trade Center in New York and the Pentagon in Washington was beyond the comprehension of so many people because the script it followed was apocalyptic, not rational. If we look at it again: there the World Trade Center, symbol of the globalized progress of the modern world, and the Pentagon, the symbol of America, the superpower – here in the kidnapped aircraft the anonymous mass murderers, executing, as they believed, the judgement of a supernatural power. Rational purposes and goals behind the assassinations cannot be discerned. The voices of Bin Laden and Mullah Omar talk about retribution for the humiliations suffered by Islam, about God's vengeance on unbelievers, and about the destruction of America. Have religious energies turned criminal here?

Ever since 11 September 2001 we have been confronted with a new quality in this active apocalyptic terrorism. A man or woman becomes an assassin for money or out of conviction, but a suicidal mass murderer becomes so only out of conviction. The Islamist terrorists evidently feel themselves to be martyrs for their faith, and are highly reverenced by the like-minded. For what conviction do they murder? For decades, fanatical masses on the streets of the Middle East have denounced the United States as 'the great Satan', and the Western world has been condemned as the corrupt 'world of unbelievers'. Materialism, pornography, the break-up of the family, and the liberation of women are only some of the accusations. Out of ignorance or self-complacency people in the West failed to take this seriously; it was ridiculed as crude and half-baked. But 'the great Satan' is nothing other than the apocalyptic 'enemy of God'. Anyone who weakens him and humiliates him is on God's side, and earns paradise. The *idée fixe* of fighting together with God in the final struggle against the godless evidently does away with every normal human inhibition about killing, heightens the ecstasy of power, and transforms suicide into an act of worship. The suicidal mass murderers of New York and Washington will have felt themselves to be as God, who in the end annihilates the godless. If they feel that they are divine executioners, they do not need a rational justification for the mass murder. The meaning of terrorism is – terror. The meaning of murder is death. After that nothing more is to follow.

No Jewish or Christian apocalyptist believed that such a destruction of other people and oneself would be followed by a new beginning, a reconstruction, or even a redemption.

The biblical apocalypses are not pessimistic scenarios of a global catastrophe which merely disseminate fear and terror so that human beings are paralysed by the corresponding belief in their doom. These apocalypses are messages of hope in danger, an encouragement to see the danger clearly and to resist it. They keep alive hope in the faithfulness of God: 'But when all these terrors of the End-time begin to take place, look up and raise your heads, because your redemption is drawing near' (Luke 21.28).

These apocalypses inculcate a realistic awareness of the dangers that threaten: 'Be afraid!' Anyone who is incapable of fear becomes blind, blind to catastrophe. But they also depict what can be seen if we 'look through the horizon', as the Indonesian word for hope puts it. 'He who endures to the end will be saved.'

The biblical apocalypses and catastrophe theologies have

nothing to do with the fantasies of global annihilation conceived by the modern prophets of disaster and the terrorists. They are teachers of hope, and say with the poet Hölderlin:

Near
and hard to grasp the God,
but where danger is, deliverance also grows.

IV

Deliver Us from Evil: God's Righteousness and Justice, and the Rebirth of Life

In order for us to be free of the evil we have brought about and which now weighs on us, we search for pardon and forgiveness of our guilt, so that we can live and breathe freely again. That isn't wrong, but it touches only one side of the evil. How can we be free, not only of the evil we have committed, but of the evil we have suffered, and cannot forget because it has left traces in body and soul? That is the other side of the evil. Here we have the perpetrators and there we have the victims – and often enough the victims become perpetrators themselves. But the two are inextricably entangled: if the victims cannot be delivered from the evil they have suffered, then the perpetrators cannot be delivered from it either. Justice must be done on both sides: the victims must receive justice, and the perpetrators must be put on the road to justice – must be set right. The way this happens through what God does is the subject of the theological doctrine of justification. Unfortunately the only question asked in the Church's tradition has always been how the guilty offenders can be set right. The fact that there must also be justice for the victims has received little attention. In this chapter I shall describe how God's righteousness and justice works on both sides – how the victims of evil receive justice, and how the perpetrators of evil are put right. That is why the chapter is not headed: 'Forgive us our trespasses', as one might expect, but 'Deliver us from evil'. In experiencing the deliverance from evil, we recognize the creative goodness of God. His justice-creating righteousness allows us to acknowledge his justice, and that makes us free for the new beginning.

The first section is a theological discussion, and it does not have to be read before the rest of the chapter can be understood. The real train of thought begins in section 2.

Critical Reservations about the Traditional Theological Interpretations of the Doctrine of Justification

1. The doctrine of justification was an issue that divided Roman Catholics and Lutherans from the sixteenth century onwards. Following extensive discussions, the final draft of an agreement was presented in January 1997, and the Joint Declaration on the Doctrine of Justification was finally signed by representatives of both churches on 31 October 1999, in Augsburg.[1]

This attempt at the end of the twentieth century to solve the controversial theological problems that had arisen over the doctrine in the Reformation period is praiseworthy as an attempt to come to terms with the past of the divided churches. But it does not in itself lead the way to a joint future. The reappraisal of what divided these churches for 400 years is no more than the precondition for a future community between them; it is not yet the community itself. If we wish to arrive at a new, common doctrine of justification in the framework of the teaching about the justification of God and human beings, we must choose a more fundamental and more comprehensive approach.

2. The Lutheran doctrine of justification was laid down in the Augsburg Confession (Article 4); the Catholic doctrine was defined by the Council of Trent (in Sessio 6). Both doctrines developed in the sixteenth century out of the practice of the sacrament of penance, and are still shackled by the conditions imposed by that framework. In the confessional, it is a matter of the admission of guilt (*confessio oris*), the contrition of the heart (*contritio cordis*), and active restitution (*satisfactio operum*), as well as the priest's releasing words of forgiveness: '*Ego absolvo te.*' It is easy to see that the theological question as to whether faith is enough, or whether works are also necessary, is really the

practical question about the conditions under which the words of absolution are to be spoken.

But the sacrament of penance is confined to the Western Church and to medieval tradition. It is foreign to the Orthodox Church, and finds hardly any support in patristic traditions, which know nothing of it in this form. Compared with the biblical ideas about God's righteousness and justice – the ideas which we find in Israel's Torah and in the Christian gospel – the medieval sacrament of penance itself, as well as the teachings about justification developed in its framework, are unfounded and untenable. Why?

(a) In the sacrament of penance, the power of evil – what we call sin – is reduced to human guilt.

(b) This sacrament has to do only with the perpetrators of evil, not the victims. The sacrament of penance is offender-orientated, and is forgetful of the victims, just like Roman law.

(c) Justification is reduced to the forgiveness of guilt, which means that it is confined to the guilty.

(d) The forgiveness of sins is based on a theology of the cross without Christ's resurrection, and this theology of the cross is reduced to a theology of satisfaction: Christ, the vicarious victim, who takes away the sins of the world.

(e) In the framework of the sacrament of penance, justification is one-sided: it is related only to the guilty person, who is to become just 'before God', who accuses him; it is not related to the God who is to be justified 'before the human beings' who accuse him.

(f) God's grace is signified through the words of absolution. But this one-sided representation reduces faith to a passive reception, robbing it of the active sanctification of God's name and the active justification of God.

(g) In considering the Latin-medieval sacrament of penance and the sixteenth-century teachings on justification, it must, in short, be said that the biblical ideas about God's saving righteousness and justice, and the believing justification of God, cannot be adequately grasped through the terminology of Roman penal law.

3. In considering the biblical basis for the doctrine of justification, we start from the following assumptions:

(a) The Pauline doctrine of justification is foreign to the sixteenth-century Lutheran and tridentine doctrines of justification, because it knows nothing of a sacrament of penance, and bases our righteousness not on Christ's cross but on his resurrection.

(b) According to the whole testimony of the New Testament, the adoption of the Pauline theology of justification is one-sided unless it is supplemented by the sanctification theology of the synoptic Gospels. Whereas the one doctrine is formulated in legalistic terms, the other may be called therapeutic.

(c) According to the whole testimony of the Bible, the Christian doctrine of God's justifying and healing righteousness must be supplemented by the Old Testament idea of justice-creating and liberating righteousness. Only the One who 'brings about justice for those who suffer violence' can also put right the perpetrators of violence.

(d) The goal of the justice-creating and justifying righteousness of God is the kingdom of God, in which God arrives at his due rights in all those he has created and in the new earth 'in which righteousness dwells' (2 Peter 3.13).

(e) This means that the lives of the righteous consist of more than just a continual, self-absorbed repentance. Their lives are filled with the sanctification of God's name, the doing of his will, the hope of his kingdom, and the glorification of his eternal Being.

The Cry for Justice

Where does the question about justice come to the surface today? And where in our own biographies do we find breaches of justice which are still unhealed? Let us look first at some personal questions and individual perspectives, and then go on to structural questions and perspectives that are supra-individual.

1. The first cry is the cry of the victims of injustice, violence and lies. Their cry to God is the cry for justice and truth. For them the question about God is identical with the question whether there is any justice in this world or not. The victims of the mass murders of the twentieth century haunt us with their cry

for justice, a cry which was so brutally smothered. In the dumb sighs of oppressed peoples we hear the hunger and thirst of men and women for a justice which for them does not exist. It is the cry out of the depths of God-forsakenness and out of an impotent subjection to the superior power of evil.

But the cry for justice and for God does not spring only out of experiences of suffering in the great crimes against humanity committed in our time. It also wells up out of the everyday experiences of being personally at the mercy of chance or blind fate, sickness and accident. Is chance just, when it lets the one person live and the other die? Is life fair, when it permits one person to grow up healthy and the other disabled? Is death just, when it allows young people full of hope to die in torment, while old people, tired of living, go on living endlessly? No, how can there be a just God when what human beings experience in life and death is not justice but merely caprice? Chance is wayward and fate is blind. The victims of injustice, violence, sickness, suffering and death torment themselves with the question: is God just?

In recent times there has been a good deal of talk in Europe and America about 'innocent victims'. But that is highly ambiguous phraseology. On the one hand the intention is to increase sympathy with the victims, but on the other the phrase implicitly declares that 'the guilty' are 'non-innocent victims' of violence. As far as the victims of injustice and violence are concerned, the category 'guilty-innocent' is irrelevant. The person who employs it justifies the violence, whether intentionally or not.

2. The second cry is the cry of the perpetrators of evil, once they become frighteningly aware that when they fell upon their victims and oppressed, humiliated or murdered them, they became the willing accomplices of evil, and were made the involuntary slaves of a rule of violence. These offenders are also the victims of evil, but unlike the suffering victims, they become the active slaves of evil, and therefore guilty. They lose their humanity, not through a suffering that sees no way out, but because of insane blindness and compulsive acts. They don't know what they are doing, and they don't want to know. They are like blind people who, because they have lost their sight, no longer see the suffering of their victims. They are like the deaf, who can no longer hear the cries of their victims because they no longer have

an ear for them. They have lost themselves and sold themselves into the slavery of evil. So they no longer feel any pangs of conscience, and are no longer themselves; their life is a lie which has become second nature. Without an identity or a name, they have done the dirty work they were given to do. The psycho-analysis of the agents and accomplices of cynical and inhuman dictators – their torturers, hangmen and spies – shows that they have lost the ability to grieve, and have therefore lost the ability to love as well. They have become living corpses.

The perpetrators of evil and those who involuntarily made possible what they did, do not hunger and thirst for God and his righteousness and justice, on the contrary: 'I hope there is no God and no divine justice', said a German officer to my father in 1944, in Russia, 'for if there is any divine justice the German people will suffer a terrible fate after this mass murder of the Jews.'[2] The victims cry to God out of their God-forsakenness, and the perpetrators cry out against God out of their godlessness: there dare not be a God, for there dare not be any justice to condemn what we have done.

The godlessness of the perpetrators doesn't show itself merely in tremendous crimes against humanity; it is manifested in all of us and in everyday life too. Our conscious willing and doing is always already conditioned by the forces we are unconscious of; and that means that willing and doing are qualified in a particular way by the things we repress because we don't want to know what they are. But what we repress is still there for all that, and it oppresses us and often enough leads to a wrongful behaviour which we did not intend. It is only 'with limited liability' and greatly 'diminished responsibility' that we are masters in our own house. On the other hand, everything we intend and do is embedded in social conditioning and historical conflicts. Things generally turn out differently from what we expected. There is 'the cussedness of things in general', there is opposition from outside, the contrariness of other people, and occasionally malicious antagonists. All these prevent us from doing what we want to do. How often do we feel bound to excuse ourselves, saying 'I didn't mean that to happen'? In other words, as perpetrators too we are at the disposal of chance or fate, 'the auspicious moment', or 'the awkward situation'. Then we talk about 'an unfortunate chain of circumstances'. It isn't difficult to understand the conflict Paul describes: 'For I do not do what I want, but I do the very thing I hate . . . I do not do the good I want, but the evil I do not want is what I do. But if I do what I do not want, it is no longer I that do it, but sin which dwells within me (Rom. 7.15, 19–20). According to the overweening human being, his free will is always at call; he controls everything and is controlled by nothing. But this is an illusion which turns men and women into 'proud and unhappy gods', as Luther said. It is more realistic to recognize in the perpetrators of evil and what they do the dependency on inner forces and outward circumstances which makes these people the slaves of evil – although this recognition does not mean excusing them or ourselves.

3. 'A man should be a shining star,
   but that is simply not the way things are.'

So wrote Bert Brecht in his *Dreigroschenoper*.[3] And it is true that we experience evil and the lie not just individually as their victims or their perpetrators, but also in the social conditions, the political structures, and the historical chances or destinies which we have not created but of which we are a part. In these structures or systems we are delivered up to forces which are certainly to an increasing degree the work of human beings, but which are nevertheless outside our own control.

There are political systems in which good things, brought about with great personal commitment, minister only to the greater evil, because they stabilize the system of injustice and organized violence. We might think of the tyrannies of the Fascist and Communist dictators, which misused the good will of many people for their own evil purposes.

There are also social systems in which what is good on the one side ministers to what is evil on the other. And there are cultural systems in which rituals which for thousands of years counted as vitally necessary, showed themselves to be institutions of evil once these systems were replaced by others. Today, for example, we view human sacrifices to the gods as cruel and terrible perversions of religion. Yet for thousands of years they were considered to be good and important factors in stabilizing the social systems in which fearful human beings lived together with the fearsome gods. In political, social and cultural systems like this, the evil is hidden in the values which are generally accepted as a matter of course, the values about which people imprisoned in the system say: this is the way it has to be; anything else is impossible. Nowadays the form this lie takes is the phrase: 'there is no alternative' – although, after all, there are always at least two possibilities. Institutionalized evil, and the lie that dominates public life, only come to the surface when there are far-reaching revolutions in the system – although this does not mean that they are then necessarily replaced by the good and the true. In revolutions of this kind, what once counted as right is shown to be manifestly wrong, and this discovery horrifies the perpetrators, who did not know what they were doing. They then either disown the acts or disown themselves.

Of course we can ironically ask: can structures repent? The answer is a simple one: of course not, just by themselves, for structures are not determining subjects. But they can be changed by human beings, because it is human beings who have made them. Consequently the institutionalized wickedness of human beings who are joined together in communities can be changed. But it is pointless to accuse systems and to persist obstinately but ineffectually in the accusation. Whether we look at the perpetrators or the victims or the system, the hardest question is always the same: it is the question about the justice of the history in which we find ourselves. If so much in our lives, in our sufferings, and in what we do, is conditioned by chance and fate, then we are obviously not living in a just world which offers equal opportunities to all and in which everyone has the same rights. Accident and fate condition each life in a different way, and this does not permit the perception of any divine justice. The victims are surrendered wretchedly to their sufferings, and the perpetrators are left alone with their guilt. Yet the cry for justice is there. It is directed against these experiences of history to which our lives are surrendered. And the cry merges with the cry of the God-forsaken for God, and of the godless against God.

To dispense with the question about the divine justice means accepting the unjust sufferings of the victims, the lawless actions of the perpetrators, and institutionalized wickedness; it means ceasing to call evil, injustice, lies and suffering by their proper names.

If there is no God, what happens to the hunger and thirst for justice in this world? If there is no God, who protests against the inhumanities in a world where God is eclipsed?

This means that evil as 'the power of sin' crosses moral bounds, spanning the guilt of the perpetrators, who have become the slaves of evil, and the suffering of those who have become evil's victims. In the history of our lives evil goes together with the sicknesses of mind and soul and the afflictions of the body on which human beings are inwardly dependent, and it is linked with the chances and the inexorable fate of history to which they are outwardly exposed. Sin is a shared 'sickness unto death'.

As powers which enslave human beings, evil and lies predominate in the political, social and cultural systems which turn human beings into perpetrators and victims, and often enough into victimized perpetrators and willing victims.

From this brief survey of life as we know it, it will be clear that it is quite inadequate to reduce the power of sin to the guilt of the perpetrators, to limit the force of divine righteousness to the forgiveness of their guilt, and to confine justification to the position of the sinner before God.

God Is Just when He Brings about Justice

Let me first explain briefly what I mean by this proposition, which I shall then go on to develop.

The God of Israel does not lay down what is right and wrong in order to repay good with good and evil with evil. He *brings about* what is right and just, where there is wrong and injustice. God is not a blind judge, like Justitia with her bandaged eyes, who judges without respect of person. God the judge is the friend at court, the advocate of the people without rights and of wrong-doers (Psalm 82). On the side of the victims his righteousness is a righteousness that brings about justice, and on the side of the offenders a righteousness that sets them on the right path. It is as the God who brings about justice and makes-just that God arrives at his rights in those he has created. And in this way, in the midst of this unjust and godless world, the kingdom of God and his righteousness already begins, a just world which is in accord with God.

The righteousness of God which brings about justice

According to the Old Testament, God's righteousness is his creative faithfulness to the community he shares, in the covenant with his people and in the covenant with his creation. According to the First Commandment, the God of Israel is the God who has freed the prisoners from their enslavement. So it is right to expect him to 'execute (create) justice for the oppressed' (Ps. 14.7; 103.6). He brings about justice for widows and orphans (Deut. 10.18; Ps. 82.3; Isa. 1.17) and is present among people who are forsaken and lost. He cares for the rights of 'strangers'. That is why anyone who cries out for God can cry with Ps. 31.1: 'In thy righteousness deliver me!' In the light of Israel's experiences of God, this justice-creating, saving and redeeming righteousness is also understood as God's compassion. But this compassion does not mean that God puts mercy before judgement, or retains for himself the sovereign right to reprieve those who have been justly condemned. It is rather that his creative and saving justice is itself his mercy. So the wretched have the right to claim his compassion, and do not have to beg and whine for mercy.[4]

Because Israel's experience of God is the experience of liberating, saving and justice-creating righteousness, this righteousness also determines Israel's hope for the world: the promised Messiah 'will judge the poor with righteousness and decide with equity for the meek of the earth' (Isa. 11.4). God's Spirit, the life-giver, 'will bring forth justice to the nations' (Isa. 42.1), and justice in nature: '. . . Then justice will dwell in the wilderness, and righteousness abide in the fruitful field, and the effect of righteousness will be peace' (Isa. 32.15f.).

By bringing about justice in this way, God reveals himself to be the just God. But his Being is not manifested only in what he does; God is also already present where injustice is suffered. If God brings about justice for those who suffer violence, then he also identifies himself with the victims of violence, putting himself on their side. What is done to the poor and helpless is indirectly done to him too. His justice-creating righteousness is intensified through his Real Presence among the victims. We find this conviction first in the ideas about the 'Shekinah', the presence of God which indwells the people of the covenant. But in a wider setting too, wherever God's intervention on behalf of the victims of injustice and violence is expected, then – as the story in Matthew 25 about the Last Judgement of the Son of man tells us – his special presence among them is also expected.

If justice is established for people without rights, then it is among them that God's righteousness and justice begins to be manifested in this world. If the just God is already present among them, then it is with them that the divine judgement begins in this world.

Jesus Christ – God's Righteousness and Justice in the World of Victims and Perpetrators

For people who believe in God for Christ's sake, God's righteousness and justice can be perceived, not from the law of the cosmos or the course of history, but from the life, self-surrender and resurrection of Christ, his presence and future. As Jesus acts, God acts too; as Jesus suffers, God suffers too; as Jesus lives, God lives too. The Gospel of John sums it up in what Jesus says about himself: 'He who sees me sees the Father', for 'I am in the Father and the Father is in me' (John 14.9, 11). Faith which makes just, and provides the grounds for a new beginning, is concrete, personal knowledge of Christ.[5]

The healing power of Jesus' earthly life, and the faith that heals

According to the synoptic Gospels, the first thing that men and women experienced about Jesus was the healing power which the sick discovered in his presence. In the nearness of 'the Son of man' who comes to seek that which is lost, men and women are shown to be not 'sinners' first of all (as they are in Paul), but people who are sick.[6] Out of the darkness into which they have been banished, so that no one is forced to see them, they come into the light of Jesus and seek the healing power of his physical presence. When he begins his public ministry, Jesus' gaze falls on the sick first of all. He understood people, whatever they might be otherwise, in their sicknesses and possession: 'That evening, at sundown, they brought to him all who were sick or possessed with demons. And the whole city was gathered together about the door. And he healed many who were sick with various diseases, and cast out many demons' (Mark 1.32–4). This healing power, must have emanated from his own vital force, as is made plain in the story about 'the woman with an issue of blood', who only came up behind him and 'touched his garment' (Mark 5.25–34). And this is the general picture we are given: 'Wherever he came, in villages, cities, or country, they laid the sick in the market places, and besought him that they might touch even the fringe of his garment; and as many as touched it were made well' (Mark 6.56; 'the fringe of his garment' being an oblique way of talking about his body).

These healings are always associated with the expulsion of 'unclean spirits', demons. This is a way of saying that Jesus' vital power was to an extraordinary degree infectious life: it was *vita vivificans* – life that gives life. When Jesus comes, life comes into a sick and frightened world. The Gospels ascribe this life-giving life of Jesus to his baptism with the Spirit. From the time of his baptism in the Jordan, Jesus was full of the life-giving Spirit of God, which 'rested' on him. God's Spirit led him and acted through him. Where this life-giving divine energy is active, the 'unclean spirits' (Mark 1.23), these demonic tormenting spirits of destruction, are forced to retreat. Men and women are restored to health and reason, once these powers are forced to leave them alone. 'Demons' are powers of breakdown and destruction, conceived of in personal terms. They are characterized by a delight in torment. When the Messiah comes and brings his messianic world, these tormenting spirits will disappear from the earth, and life will be again as sound and as much worth living and loving as God created it to be.

Miraculous healings were common enough in the ancient

world. Jesus' healings have therefore been interpreted as belonging to the category of the old ideas about the 'God-man', or have been viewed in terms of modern miracle healers. But according to the New Testament interpretations, Jesus' healings belong to a different context. They are part of the coming of God's kingdom and his righteousness. When the eternally living God comes to those he has created, the forces of destruction are forced to retreat. The kingdom of the living God drives out the germs of death and disseminates the seeds of life. The kingdom of God which is present in the person of Jesus doesn't just bring salvation in the religious sense; it brings healing holistically. The kingdom is experienced in the recovery of health in both body and soul. In the healings of the sick the righteousness of God which sets things right is experienced physically.

When God comes and puts to rights this world which has been destroyed by godless powers, this is not something miraculous or out of the way; it is a matter of course. It is just what could be expected. In the context of biblical interpretations, Jesus' healings are 'miracles of the kingdom'. In the daybreak colours of the new creation of all things, they are really not miracles at all; they are that which is then bound to come. It is only when the great hope for the approaching new creation of all things comes to be lost, and when the future is no longer anticipated, that these stories about healings seem like 'miracles' in an unchanged world. But in the framework of hope for the coming of God and his kingdom, Jesus' healings become inextinguishable reminders of this future.

Just as severe illnesses are fore-tokens of death, we can understand Jesus' healings of the sick as fore-tokens too. They foreshadow the resurrection and eternal life. It is only when this frail, mortal life is reborn to a life that is eternal and will not pass away that what Jesus did for the sick and possessed in his own time will be completed. In that resurrection world, the kingdom of God will be consummated, the kingdom whose seeds Jesus has planted in our minds through his words and in our bodies through his healing power. If we think of sickness the kingdom of God means healing. If we think of death it means resurrection.

All Christian missionary and revival movements were also movements of healing, and still are. The gospel that awakens

faith is always accompanied by healing 'signs and wonders'.
Healings brought about by the Spirit in the name of Jesus and
the exorcism of demons in the sign of his cross accompany the
mission and spread of Christianity. So Christianity at its very
heart has to be described as 'the mission of the Spirit', and its
message, as Pope John Paul II said, must be called 'the gospel of
life'.

Yet the healing power which radiated from Jesus' life is only
one of the causes of the healings we are told about. Jesus evidently did not have this healing power at his own, free disposal.
In some circumstances these healings happened, in others not. In
his home town Nazareth 'he could do no mighty work', we are
told in Mark 6.5. So we have to ask: under what conditions did
Jesus' healing power act?

When a sick boy is brought to him, Jesus beseeches the father:
'If you could only believe! All things are possible to him who
believes.' The father answers, with tears: 'I believe, Lord, help
my unbelief' (Mark 9.23f.). This little bit of unbelieving belief is
enough: Jesus lifts the boy up 'and he arose'. To the woman 'with
an issue of blood', who extorted her healing from him without
his will, he also said: 'My daughter, your faith has made you
whole. Go in peace.' So before healings can take place the healing faith of the sick person must be added to the healing power
of Jesus

What kind of faith is this? It is evidently a faith without
specific articles of faith, and without a specific object – that is to
say, it is a kind of absolute faith. What is meant is not explicitly
the faith of Israel, nor is it the Christian faith in Jesus. From the
contexts of the relevant texts we can deduce that what is meant
is a singular belief in possibility: 'All things are possible to him
that believes' for 'with God all things are possible' (Mark 9.23).
This is a human trust which in the presence of God's wealth of
possibilities bursts through all earthly and human boundaries
and the limitations which sickness imposes, and sets reality, in
whatever way it is limited, within God's unlimited wealth of
possibility. Because believers and those who trust in God place
the restrictions of their personal reality within God's wealth of
possibility, for them the healing power of Jesus becomes possible. If all the things that are possible to God are possible to the

person who believes, then people who believe, themselves acquire a share in the unlimited possibility of God. If this is not to be a self-deification, it has to be the power of the divine Spirit which indwells these people and is hidden in them which awakens such an absolute faith in possibility. Healings of the sick and the liberation of the possessed therefore take place where the healing power of the divine Spirit in the life of Jesus meets the power of faith in the person who is sick – that is to say when the Spirit's efficacy and the recipient's trust in possibility come together. Through their faith, the sick make it possible for Jesus to heal them.

The justice-creating solidarity of Jesus with the victims of evil

To the sick Jesus brought the healing power of the Spirit, and similarly to those without their just rights and to the unjust he brought God's justice. This is manifested in his community with 'tax-collectors and sinners', as these people are called in the synoptic Gospels. Jesus demonstrated this community so publicly that his critics said: 'This man receives sinners and eats with them' (Luke 15.2). That does not mean that Jesus 'had got into bad company', but rather that with these people, whom their society had rejected and pushed out, he was anticipating God's messianic banquet with the nations. There is no way of understanding the symbolic act of his eating and drinking with 'tax-collectors and sinners' except in the context of his proclamation that 'the kingdom of God has come to you'.

We shall not begin our account of 'the justification of sinners' with Paul's Epistle to the Romans, but shall start instead with the realistic presentation of 'tax-collectors and sinners' in the synoptic Gospels. In the Gospel accounts, not all are sinners alike, and not all sinners are alike, as Rom. 3.23 maintains. The group who are described as 'tax-collectors and sinners' were people who because of their poverty or their unsavoury activity were unable to keep God's law, and were therefore rejected and excluded by 'the good people'. To be despised and excluded is deeply wounding to a person's self-respect. It is often the case

that because of social pressure rejected people take the judgement of others on board themselves, and begin to despise and
hate themselves. They have no confidence in themselves. We can
see this today among people who have been made the underdogs
and losers in the social survival of the fittest. People who in this
situation find someone who accepts them and affirms them,
because he or she respects them, and hopes they can make a new
beginning, feel that they have been given fresh heart and are as if
redeemed. They again trust themselves to do things which they
had long since given up. Jesus' acceptance of 'tax-collectors and
sinners' is their social healing. In addition it is the assertion of
God's justice-creating righteousness among these victims of a
self-righteous society. In this way Jesus brings the kingdom of
God and his righteousness into the underworld of the humiliated
and the insulted, and throws open the inner spiritual prisons of
their self-contempt.

But where on the one side we find excluded and despised
people such as these 'tax-collectors and sinners', we find on the
other the righteous and the good, who decide what is to count as
right and good in society, and determine the people who must
therefore be viewed as wrong and wicked. Just as it is the possession of riches which turns poor people into 'the poor', it is the
possession of the good which turns the others into 'the wicked'.
When Jesus accepts sinners and eats with them, he is then bound
to appear to the good people of his time either as a sinner himself
or as a revolutionary, who wants to turn their values upside
down. But by accepting sinners Jesus saves the righteous and
good too: he saves them from their self-righteousness. The
person who accepts even 'sinners' is also prepared to accept 'the
righteous' – though not in their self-righteousness, but as sinners
in the fellowship with tax-collectors and sinners which they had
broken off. It is one and the same justice which by bringing about
justice saves the one and judges the other, so as to bring them all
together into community with God.

The passion of Jesus: his way to the victims of evil

This is solidarity christology: Christ with us, the God-forsaken. The Gospels describe Jesus' passion as the story of his path into an ever-deeper self-emptying. This path ends with his execution on the Roman cross. In the life of Jesus we can see a clear pull downwards. It is the pull of self-giving love. The Eros of the ancient world was a love for the beautiful and radiant. But Jesus' love turned to the sick, the victims of violence and little un-noticeable people. Jesus evidently saw the helpless as important, and people who were shut out by the world as called by God; we can see this from the Beatitudes in the Sermon on the Mount. To these people, to whom society held out no future, he proclaimed the future of the kingdom of heaven. Here, 'the devil takes the hindmost' gives way to 'the last shall be first'.

It is obvious that 'the first' – the powerful people of this world – were bound to react to this radical revaluation of their values with persecution, humiliation and execution. 'The cross is the world's answer to Christian love', said Ernst Bloch rightly.[7] But in taking his way to the cross, Jesus was also making his own decision: his active love for sufferers becomes his suffering love with sufferers. We understand his suffering obedience to God not as his sacrifice for the sins of the world but as his unreserved self-giving to the uttermost for the God-forsaken. Here Jesus reveals a love on God's part 'such as was never thought of in any God', as Bloch said. The Godness of God manifested in Jesus' surren-der of himself to death on the cross is a love which is capable not only of suffering but even of the fate of death. So from this 'love of God which is in Christ Jesus' (Rom 8.39) even 'tribulation, distress, persecution, famine or sword' can no longer separate us (8.35). Paul's hymn of praise in Rom. 8.31–9 to God's uncon-querable love is a hymn of praise to the self-giving love in which Jesus and God are wholly and entirely one.

If God goes where Jesus goes, if God himself was in Jesus, then through his passion Jesus brings the love of God to people who are as cast down and emptied as he was himself. His cross stands between the countless crosses which line the bloody path of the tyrants and men of violence in human history, from Spartacus to the concentration and death camps of the German Hitler tyranny, to the 'disappeared' of the Latin American military dictatorships, and the liquidated in the Gulag Archipelago of the Soviet imperium.

This means that the sufferings of Jesus' self-giving are not his sufferings only. They are inclusive, comprehending the sufferings of all the God-forsaken in this world; they are the sufferings he shares with all the suffering. By virtue of his self-giving he becomes their brother. His cross is a brother's cross that stands among the crosses of this world, as a sign – yes, as a revelation – that God himself participates in our pain, and that he is beside us in our forsakenness. Paul Gerhardt brought this out in his moving verses:

> And when I am departing,
> then part not thou from me;
> When mortal pangs are darting,
> come, Lord, and set me free!
> And when my heart must languish
> amidst the final throe,
> release me from mine anguish
> by thine own pain and woe.[8]

In his solidarity with them, the assailed and dying Christ becomes the comfort of assailed and dying men and women. In their deadly fear, his fear and suffering become their comfort, for where Christ is, there is God.[9] In surrendering himself to a God-forsaken death, Christ brought God to the God-forsaken. Jesus entered into his humiliation and his forsakenness by God and human beings so that he could be a brother to the forsaken, and be beside them as their friend in their time of need. Ultimately he helps them not through supernatural miracles but, by virtue of his self-giving, through his pain: 'Through his wounds we are healed' (Isa. 53.5; Matt. 8.17) – healed from our sickness unto death, the God-forsakenness which is also called sin, inasmuch as sin means separation.

'Only the suffering God can help', wrote Dietrich Bonhoeffer in his Gestapo cell.[10] A God who by reason of his essence cannot suffer, cannot suffer with us either, or even feel sympathy. The *Deus impassibilis* is a God without a heart and without compassion, a cold heavenly power.[11] The God whose divinity Jesus revealed through his self-giving always helps first of all by suffering with us. For forsaken human beings he becomes their companion in suffering.

This was the conversion experience of the 59-year-old Archbishop Oscar Arnulfo Romero: 'In all the crucified of history the crucified God became present to him . . . In the eyes of the poor and oppressed of his people he saw the disfigured face of God', wrote his biographer Jon Sobrino.[12]

It is only Jesus' identification with the victims of sin through his giving of himself to them which explains the tremendous drama of the great Judgement of the Son of man pictured in Matt. 25.31–46 and makes it comprehensible. The point is not the judgement in accordance with good or bad works. It is the identification of the coming Son of man with the hungry and thirsty, the strangers, the naked, the sick and the imprisoned: 'As you did it not to one of the least of these my brothers, you did it not to me', for 'I was hungry . . . thirsty . . . sick' and so forth. In Jesus' giving of himself to these 'least', the Son of man-Judge of the world is already present. He identifies with these victims of human history to such a degree that he will judge according to what was done to him – or not done to him – in them. He judges the perpetrators of injustice not each individually, in accordance with their breach of the law (as is the practice in our criminal law); he judges them in the face of their victims. He judges between the perpetrators and the victims. The victims become the judges of the offenders, because in the Son of man-Judge of the world the victims with whom he identifies himself encounter the perpetrators.

Jesus' representation for those enslaved by evil

This is representation christology: Christ for us – the godless. According to Israel's Torah, 'sinners' are the people who break the law or are without the law. But in his Epistle to the Romans Paul starts from the assumption that 'all men, both Jews and Greeks, are under the power of sin' (3.9). As we see from his account in Galatians 2 of his meeting with Peter, Paul goes beyond the concept of sin which makes the Torah its yardstick, expanding the boundaries so that he can pass on the saving and justifying gospel to all human beings, Jews and Gentiles alike. 'We ourselves are Jews by birth and not Gentile sinners, yet we know that a person is justified not by works of the law but through faith in Jesus Christ. And we have come to believe in Christ Jesus so that we might be justified by faith in Christ, and not by doing the works of the law, because no one will be justified by the works of the law' (Gal. 2.15f., following New RSV). Paul takes as his premise a universal concept of sin so that he can proclaim the gospel universally; and this means that for him the power of sin (to which all human beings have become subject) must have existed before Israel's election and its Law, and must as 'the sickness unto death' have spread godless death. So sin must be a perversion of human beings as they were first created, a perversion through which they have lost the radiance of God's glory (Rom. 3.23).

But does this mean that all human beings are sinners without distinction, in the sense that they are all perpetrators of sin and therefore in the thrall of evil? It is true that Paul does not distinguish specially between the perpetrators and the victims of evil, for he sees the perpetrators only as 'slaves of sin', who are bound to do what they do without any freedom of their own. This does not excuse them, however; on the contrary, it puts them in need of their own particular salvation. They cannot conquer the sin to which they have become subject, either through their own strength, or with the help of divine grace. They can only 'die to sin', so that for this godless power they are dead; and this being so, the godless power loses its right to them.

The righteousness of God which the gospel brings into this world, subject as it has become to the power of sin, is not a 'righteousness which holds good before God', as Luther put it, but the 'justifying righteousness' of God himself, who proves himself to the unrighteous as the righteous one, and asserts his rights in his unrighteous created beings.

Let us first ask here about the christological foundation for this divine righteousness which 'justifies the ungodly' (Rom. 4.5).

Paul sees this in the events of the self-surrender and raising of Jesus, 'who was put to death for our trespasses and raised for our justification' (Rom. 4.25). The forgiveness of our sins belongs within the sufferings and death of Christ 'for us', but it is only with the raising of Christ 'for us' that our justification becomes manifest. The justification of sinners is therefore only completed in the raising of Christ and the rebirth to eternal life which it throws open for us.

How can sins 'be forgiven'? No one can ever undo something that has once been done. All guilt chains the present to the past, robbing it of its freedom for the future. No good deed ever compensates for an evil one. The perpetrators, indeed, have only short memories, because they repress what weighs on them; but the memories of their victims are long, because they bear the scars of their suffering for the rest of their lives. Consequently the perpetrators are dependent on their victims if they are to be liberated. 'Expiation' is supposed to restore the universal order of things which has been impaired, and lift the burden of guilt from the offender. But expiation is not humanly possible, because the wrong that has been committed remains; what is done is done. Only God himself can liberate someone from the burden of guilt for what is past, and give life a new beginning. He does this by taking his judgement about the wrong of sin upon himself, in order to give his creative 'justification of life' to people who have become subject to this sin.

In the story of Noah and the Flood, we find the idea about God's pain and regret – in Hosea the idea of God's 'repentance' – in the Psalms the cry for the power of God's compassion.

Let us look at the image of God's pain. The suffering of God is important both for the victims of sin and for those who are enslaved by sin. To perceive this suffering releases the victims from the torment of remembrance, and frees the enslaved from the power of their repressions. Even God cannot make what is done undone, but he can loose the fetters which bind the present to this past, and open for the present a new future.

The pain of God is revealed in Jesus' passion and death. It is the pain of God's infinite love, which is manifested in Jesus' self-giving. This has often been interpreted to mean that Jesus died as the vicarious victim for our sins, paying off our debts in a heavenly bank, so to speak, and transferring them from us to him. But this is just what it does not mean. Interpretations of this kind are only illustrations – more or less apt images – but they do not touch the heart of the matter. The one who 'was put to death for our trespasses' (Rom. 4.25) was not the one sacrificed for our sins by God, his Father; he is the one who was sent by his Father to those who had been given up for lost (Rom. 1.24, 26, 28), so that God himself might be brought into the pit of God-forsakenness and could thereby awaken these godless people for a new beginning. Consequently it is often misleading to talk about 'our sins' in the plural, as if, well-meaning though we really are, we have unfortunately made a number of mistakes, which must be forgiven us because we have already forgiven ourselves. This is the way some politicians today talk about their 'mistakes'. Sins in the plural may be 'forgiven', but the sinner, in the singular of his or her personhood, must be 'accepted', so as to die to sin and be born anew; it is this that is symbolized by baptism, in the community of Christ (Rom. 6). The personal 'for us' of Christ is primary; the objective 'for our sins' is secondary.

The Resurrection of Christ with the Victims and Perpetrators of Evil

The solidarity of the crucified Christ with the victims of evil is only the first step to their liberation. The forgiveness of the guilt of the perpetrators is no more than the precondition for their rebirth to true life. To reduce the event of justification to the forgiveness of guilt (a reduction suggested by the medieval sacrament of penance and the Lutheran doctrine of the Augsburg Confession Article IV) is misleading and wrong. According to Paul, Christ was indeed 'put to death for our trespasses' but he was 'raised for our justification' (Rom. 4.25). For Augustine, what corresponds to Christ's real death is the real forgiveness of sins in us, and what corresponds to his true resurrection is our true justification.[13] The 'salvific meaning' of his suffering and his death certainly lies in the forgiveness of our guilt, but this does not yet cover the salvific meaning which is described through the terms 'justification' or 'our righteousness'. That emerges only as the salvific meaning of his resurrection.

It is therefore Christ's resurrection from the dead which reveals the saving significance of his death on the cross.[14] Moreover the resurrection does not mean only that God 'identifies' himself with the crucified Jesus. The resurrection is a separate and special act of God's,[15] through which the new world of eternal life is thrown open for the victims and perpetrators of evil. For the resurrection of Christ is not exclusively his private affair. Rather, he has been raised inclusively, as the head of the new humanity and as the first-born of the whole creation. Through Christ's resurrection from the dead we God-forsaken and Godless 'dead' are born again to a living hope (1 Peter 1.3). It is only this that brings us into the sphere of life of the divine righteousness. In the light of Christ's resurrection, the positive side of the divine compassion with the victims and perpetrators of sin becomes manifest. In the forgiveness of guilt God's concern is not the guilt itself; it is the new life to which he desires to awaken the guilty. It is not the person whose guilt is forgiven who is already justified; it is only the person who is born again to new life out of the Spirit of the resurrection. What is positive does not emerge of itself out of the negation of the negative; the negation of the negative is no more than the precondition for the new beginning.

The resurrection of Christ, then, must not be reduced to the revelation of the salvific significance of the cross, and in the same way there is no equal weight between Christ's death and resurrection, and consequently no equal weight either between the forgiveness of guilt and the rebirth of life. 'How much more', says Paul, when he is talking about the Christ who died and was raised (Rom. 8.34). The raising of Christ from death is an expression of the surplus of grace, for 'where sin abounded, grace abounded all the more' (Rom. 5.20). This added-value of grace becomes effective when liberation from the chains which bind the victims and the guilty to the past allows them to move out into the new shared life in the powers of God's righteousness.

A one-sided theology of the cross led in Lutheranism to a reduction of the experience of God's justice-creating righteousness to the forgiveness of sins, while in medieval Catholicism, similarly, it kept the sense of guilt alive in men and women in order to make them dependent on the means of grace offered by the Church. It was only in the Christianity of the seventeenth century that the rebirth to a new, independent life out of the Spirit of the resurrection came to be perceived and realized as the goal of the forgiveness of sins. It is only by experiencing the rebirth to a living hope that people become the determining subjects of their own lives with God and the world. It is only then that they 'come of age' as Christians.

When we talk about experiencing justification in faith, what we have ahead of us is not the experience of a moment; it is a dynamic process, orientated towards the future:

1. Christ comes into this world, heals the sick through his physical presence and drives out demons: that is the healing power of his lived life.
2. In his passion, Christ takes his path to the cross of the tyrants, and through his solidarity brings God to the God-forsaken: that is the consolation of the death he suffered.
3. Through the representative power of his suffering and death, he looses the chains of guilt which bind the perpetrators to their evil acts, and liberates them from the burden of their guilt.
4. Through the living power of his resurrection, he brings victims and perpetrators into a just community with God and with one another. In his rule they can live, for it extends to the living and the dead and withdraws all claims from the powers of evil.
5. With the rule of Christ, God's new creation already begins in the midst of the world of death. It is fulfilled when 'the kingdom' is handed over to God, so that the goal is reached and 'God will be all in all' (1 Cor. 15.28).

The Right of Inheritance of God's Children

A last, hidden and hence often overlooked dimension of the event of justification between the forgiveness of guilt and the rebirth to new life is to be found in the experience of God's Spirit. Seized by the Spirit of life, believers experience that, unacceptable though they are, they are accepted by God. They are no longer viewed as the victims or slaves of sin. They are accepted as God's children, and are 'born' anew from God's life-giving Spirit. They become sisters and brothers of Christ, the Son of God, who has been appointed 'the first-born among many brothers and sisters' (Rom. 8.29). 'All who are led by the Spirit of God are children of God' (Rom. 8.14).

To be children of God does not just mean that believers have conferred on them the nobility of their divine birth, so that they are given a new self-confidence, which puts them above the world. This relationship goes together with a new law: the right of inheritance. This dimension of the justification of men and women is almost entirely missing from the traditional doctrines of justification: they always talk only about God's grace. But those who are justified become 'heirs of God and fellow heirs with Christ' (Rom. 8.17). What is this 'inheritance' to which they are now legally entitled? It is the kingdom of God's glory, which brings eternal life, and will create a new heaven and a new earth on which 'righteousness dwells' (Gal. 3.29; James 2.5; Titus 3.7). To put it in legal terms, justification is on the one hand the forgiveness of guilt, and on the other the installation of human beings in their right to inherit the kingdom of God. The new right of God's children to inherit God's future opens to the people who, as victims or slaves of evil, have come to the end, the prospect of a new future with God, which also means a truly new beginning of life here and now.

The Justification of God

Wherever God brings about justice for the *victims* of injustice and violence, these are given fresh heart, and God manifests himself to them as the just God. God himself arrives at his rights in them. That is the first justification of God in this world. For that reason the people concerned will acknowledge God to be a just God.[16]

Wherever God puts the *slaves* of injustice right, by loosing the chains of the guilt which binds them to the past, and when he throws open a new beginning for their lives, he shows himself to them as the just God. God arrives at his rights in them. That is the second justification of God in this world. For that reason the people justified will acknowledge God to be a just God.

In these two modes of justice, the justice that creates and the justice that puts right, the Creator makes good his claim to those he has created. He frees them from the 'godless ties of this world', as the Barmen Theological Declaration of the Confessing Church in Germany declared in 1934, in its second thesis, and arrives at his rights in them. Through the justice that creates and puts right, God anticipates the justice and righteousness of his coming kingdom through which he will redeem the world, and in this way he justifies himself to the world. That is the third justification of God in this world. Those who experience his justice in this way, whether they are the victims or perpetrators of sin, or both at once, acknowledge his righteousness in the world by acknowledging that God is just.

God justifies us, and we justify God. That is the active and the passive justification of God. That is what justifying faith is about.

Justifying faith is not just a faith through which human beings are justified; it is a faith through which God is justified too. If we acknowledge that God is right, then we are putting the powers of evil in the world in the wrong. If we acknowledge that God is right then we also put ourselves in the wrong, if we have become subject to the fascination or the banality of evil.

If we acknowledge that God is just, then all our self-righteousness ceases. We no longer need to prove ourselves to ourselves and other people, for there is no longer any accusation. We are accepted by God, affirmed and loved, and are hence God's children, whatever achievements we have to show, or whatever mistakes. God justifies us so that we may justify him. That is the sanctification of his Name. That is the fulfilment of the First Commandment.

In the final sentence of his *Spirit of Utopia,* Ernst Bloch puts it as follows 'Only the wicked exist through their God, but the righteous – God exists through them, and in their hands is laid the sanctification of the Name, the name of God itself.'[17] That is our justification of God in the world.

V

The Spirituality of the Wakeful Senses

This call runs like a scarlet thread through Jewish and Christian writings:

Watch and Pray, Pray and Watch!

What else is Christian spirituality but this watching and praying, praying watchfully and watching prayerfully? Prayer never stands by itself. It is always bound up with watching. Here I want to talk about the watching to which true prayer is supposed to lead us. To pray is good, but to watch is better.

Modern men and women think that people who pray no longer belong properly to this world at all. They already have one foot in the world beyond. Only work helps, not prayer. Strong men often think that praying is something for old women who have nothing left to them but the rosary or the hymnbook. For most people, the notion that praying has something to do with watching, with attentiveness, and the expectation of life is a pretty strange idea.

It is true enough that our body language when we pray certainly doesn't suggest particular watchfulness. We close our eyes, and look into ourselves, so to speak. We fold our hands, so as to collect our thoughts. We lower our eyes, kneel down – even cast ourselves down with our faces to the ground. No one who sees us then would get the impression that this is a collection of especially watchful people. Isn't it rather blind trust in God which is expressed in attitudes of prayer like this? Why do we shut our eyes? Why do we crouch down and make ourselves smaller than we are? Don't we much more need to pray open-eyed, and with our heads held high? But if we are to watch, who is it that we are supposed to guard? And for whom are we supposed to be on the watch? Whom are we supposed to expect?

'Could You Not Watch with Me One Hour?'

The most arresting story about watching is also the story of Jesus' hardest hour, the night in Gethsemane. The heading in Luther's Bible is: 'The Struggle in Gethsemane'; for this is Jesus' inner struggle with God-forsakenness. His prayer to the God he trustfully calls Abba, dear Father, is not answered. The cup of eternal death does not pass him by. The night of what Martin Buber called the eclipse of God falls on him and on those who are his, and on this world. It corresponds to the dark night of the soul, in which all bearings are lost, and every feeling dries up. That is why in this hour Christ began 'to be greatly distressed and troubled', says Mark, 'to be sorrowful and troubled', writes Matthew. 'My soul is very sorrowful, even to death', he tells the disciples. At other times, Jesus had often withdrawn at night and prayed by himself in the hills. But in this hour he is afraid of being alone with his God, so he begs his disciples: 'Stay here and watch.' Jesus prays, and struggles with the dark and threatening will of his God, and his disciples are supposed to take over the watching which belongs to prayer.

But no: Jesus enters this eclipse of God praying and watching, and struggles through it: 'Not my will but yours be done.' But his disciples fall into a deep, oblivious sleep. 'Simon Peter, are you asleep? Could you not watch with me one hour?' This scene, so saddening for Jesus and so shaming for the disciples, is repeated three times: Jesus wrestles, watching, with the dark side of God – and the stifling unconsciousness of sleep descends on the disciples until the night is past and the day of Golgotha begins, into which Jesus goes resolutely: 'Get up, let us be going. My betrayer is at hand.' We all know what happens after that. But what strange kind of sleep was this, which overcame even the truest of the true?

In the monastery of Santa Croce in Florence, my wife and I discovered a remarkable fresco in one of the cells, painted by Fra Angelico. It is the scene in Gethsemane. Jesus is praying, the disciples are sleeping; but two people are watching at Jesus' side, two women. The one is looking wide-eyed in the direction of Jesus as he prays. The other is reading the Bible. It is Martha and Mary. These two women are watching with Jesus, and over him, in the hour of his God-forsakenness, just as the women later look on from afar at his cucifixion, and watch over him, after the disciples have run away.

Why do the disciples fall asleep? If the Master whom they have followed without fear and trembling begins 'to tremble and fear' himself, some cruel and inscrutable danger must surely be lurking.

What danger? Through his healings of the sick, Jesus had communicated the nearness of God in ways that could be seen and felt – through the senses. But for the disciples this nearness now evidently gives way to a feeling that God is far away. Their sense of having been found by God switches over into a feeling of complete lostness, without anything to cling to. It is as if they have been felled by some blow. Their reaction is numbness, and the sleep of hopelessness. We know what this is like too. Impending danger can stimulate us. But danger where there is no way out numbs us, and the best we can do is to take refuge in sleep, a sleep which protects us from what is unendurable. It is not a natural, refreshing sleep. It is the petrifying of all our senses, which makes us sick. Our eyes are open, but we no longer see anything. Our ears are open, but we are deaf and hear nothing. We are completely apathetic, alive but petrified. When deadly danger of this kind threatens, we involuntarily 'play dead'.

Spiritual Paralyses Today

The paralysing sleep which fell on Jesus' disciples in the night of God in Gethsemane was not their problem only. Spiritual paralyses are our problem today too.[1] How do we react to unknown dangers?

For millions of years, our consciousness has learnt to react to the most widely differing dangers in life-supporting ways. How? Through the fear which keeps us wakeful and all our senses keyed up, so that we can counter the dangers we are aware of in good time and appropriately. In all our civilizations there are inbuilt securities for our survival with which we ward off dangers we are aware of, whether it be dykes against storm tides or lightning conductors.

But today there are dangers which are present without our perceiving them. In 1986, in the catastrophe in the Chernobyl nuclear power station, deadly radioactivity was released which no one can either smell or taste or see. It has contaminated huge stretches of country in White Russia and the Ukraine, and up to now has cost the lives of more than 100,000 people. In these nuclear dangers our senses let us down. Our highly developed danger-antennae can't pick up these radioactive perils. 'Our nuclear power stations are completely safe', we are told, year for year. But no insurance company is prepared to insure a nuclear power plant against a meltdown.

The climatic changes are much more threatening than we could conceive of up to now. According to the Third Report of the International Panel of Climate Change (2001), global warming must definitely be put down to human activity. In the next 40 years the atmosphere is going to warm up by 3–5°C. Ocean levels are rising, there will be more and more 'natural' catastrophes – catastrophes which are in fact not natural but of our own making. It has been calculated that in the year 2050 there will be about 150 million climate refugees. But the President of the United States, George W. Bush, is not prepared to sign the Kyoto Protocol, so as not to endanger 'the American way of life', which, as we know, is characterized by its extensive use of energy and even more extensive atmospheric pollution. Our eyes are open but we don't see; our ears are open but we don't hear. And when the catastrophe overtakes us we will swear: 'But all this is completely new to us!'

But this means that we no longer perceive the real world. We see only our dreams, and think that our wishful thinking about reality is reality itself. But this again means that we don't live wakefully in reality; we are asleep in the agreeable dreams of our fantasy world.

What is especially seductive and spell-binding about this dream world of ours is our picture of ourselves, our cherished self-image. We see ourselves as we should like to be. Like the mirror in the fairytale, the 'Mirror, mirror on the wall' is supposed to tell us that we are 'the fairest one of all' – or the strongest, or the cleverest, or whatever pleases us best. But then there come moments of profound horror when we see ourselves reflected in the eyes of other people, and especially in the eyes of the victims. This external perspective may be painful, and hurt the image of ourselves we cherish so much; but it helps us to wake up out of our dreams and to face up to reality.

Praying and Awakening

My old Bible lexicon tells me that 'watching discerns the danger – praying brings help from God'. That may well be true, but then what comes first – the watching and then the praying, or the praying and then the waking up?

What are we seeking when we pray?

When we pray, what we are seeking is not our own wishes; we are seeking the reality of God, and are breaking out of the Hall of Mirrors of our own illusory wishes, in which we have been imprisoned. That means that we wake up out of the petrifications and numbness of our feelings. We burst apart the armour of the apathy which holds us in an iron grasp. If when we pray we seek the reality of God's world (as with the first petition of the Lord's Prayer), then prayer is the exact opposite of 'the opium of the people'. On the contrary, prayer is more like the beginning of a cure for the numbing addictions of the secular world.

In prayer we wake up to the world as it is spread out before God in all its heights and depths. We perceive the sighing of creation, and hear the cries of the created victims that have fallen dumb. We also hear the song of praise of the blossoming spring, and feel the divine love for everything that lives. So prayer to God awakens all our senses and alerts our minds and spirits.

The person who prays, lives more attentively.

Pray wakefully – that is only possible if we don't pray mystically with closed eyes, but messianically, with eyes wide open for God's future in the world. Christian faith is not blind trust. It is the wakeful expectation of God which draws in all our senses.

The early Christians prayed standing, looking up, with arms outstretched and eyes wide-open, ready to walk or to leap forward. We can see this from the pictures in the catacombs in Rome. Their posture reflects tense expectation, not quiet heart-searching. It says: we are living in God's Advent. We are on the watch, in expectation of the One who is coming, and with tense attentiveness we are going to meet the coming God.

Pray and awake. It is the ancient wisdom of the masters of prayer and meditation that it is good to pray in the morning, at the dawn of the day, in the hour between sleeping and waking, and to prepare ourselves for the reality of God and his world. This praying and awakening reveals to our lives the daybreak colours of the future, and leads to the call of Jesus: 'Get up, let us be going.' Let us wake up and see what God is bringing on this new day.

'Watch and be sober' (1 Thess. 5.6, 8). That is the next charge we hear. Sober people are not intoxicated, and don't suffer from hallucinations; they are under no illusions. When sobriety is added to the wakefulness that comes from praying, we shan't fool ourselves, and shan't let ourselves be fooled, either by political propaganda or by the consumerism thrust on us by the advertisers. We shall accept reality for what it is, and shall expose ourselves to it both in its workaday guise and in its surprises. Then we shall discover that reality is far more multi-coloured and fantastic than all our fantasies. But we shall perceive too that the pain which reality imposes on us is still, at all events, better than the self-immunizations with which we try to protect ourselves, but through which we in fact wall ourselves in.

But in German the word for 'sober' can also mean 'empty' – an empty stomach. People who are 'sober' in this sense begin the day hungry. If we are sober in this sense, we are hungry for reality, for God is in the reality. One single experienced reality is richer than a thousand dreamed-of possibilities. That is why sober contact with reality is so important. It is achieved only by the wakeful, the sober and the hungry.

Watch and expect. When we wake up in the morning we expect the new day; and in the same way, the waking which springs from prayer to God also leads to the expectation of God in the life we experience. I wake up, and open all my senses for life – for the fulfilments and for the disappointments, for what is painful as well as for what gives joy. I expect the presence of God in everything I meet and everything I do. His history with me, and with us, is an on-going history. There is nothing more exhilarating than to experience this life-history with God in full awareness. What does God have in mind for me? What does God expect of me? What is he saying to me through the things that are happening in my world, and what is my response? People who know that there is someone who is waiting for them and expecting them never give themselves up. And we are expected.

Watch and see. Strangely enough, watching and praying have very little to do with faith, but everything to do with seeing. Israel's Wisdom already knew long ago that 'the hearing ear and the seeing eye, the Lord has made them both' (Prov. 20.12). 'Seeing, they do not see', complains Jesus about his contemporaries, according to Matt. 13.13, and 'hearing they hear not. They understand nothing.' He meant the presence of the kingdom of God which he was bringing among them. But he means his own presence among us today too. According to the image of the great Judgement which we find in Matthew 25, the Son of man-Judge of the world will say: 'I was hungry and you gave me no food, I was thirsty and you gave me no drink, I was a stranger and you did not welcome me . . . Then they will answer, "Lord, when did we *see* you hungry or thirsty or a stranger or sick?" Then he will answer them, "What you did to one of the least of these, you did to me."' So the important thing is the *seeing*.

How do we learn to have seeing eyes for this presence of Christ among us? Where are our eyes opened? Archbishop Oscar Arnulfo Romero was a faithful churchman, an 'insider' familiar with the Church. When he was 59 years old he had a conversion experience: he was converted from the Church to the kingdom of God. In the poor among his people he discovered the path of faith to God in the world. 'In the faces of the poor he glimpsed the disfigured face of God', writes his biographer, Jon Sobrino. Romero put himself on the side of the poor, and a short time afterwards was shot in front of the altar in his church in El Salvador, at the orders of the rich.

To go through life with open eyes, to discern Christ in unimportant people and, alert, to do the right thing at the right time: that is what praying and watching is about. We believe so that we can see – and can withstand what we see.

'Watchman, What of the Night?'

Darkness – night – these are always symbols for the God-forsakenness of the world as well, and for the lostness of men and women. In the darkness we see nothing, and no longer know where we are. There is an apt passage in the book of Isaiah: in exile and far from home, strangers among strangers, the Israelite prisoners come to the prophet and ask: 'Watchman, what of the night?' – how long will the night last? The watchman answers: 'The morning is coming but it is still night. If you will enquire, come back again' (Isa. 21.12).

But Paul, Christ's witness, proclaims: 'The night is far gone, the day is at hand. Let us then cast off the works of darkness and put on the armour of light' (Rom. 13.12). So it is time to get up from sleep, to forget the dreams and the night terrors, and to experience life in the light of God's new day, which is now dawning.

In our dreams, each of us is alone. But when we wake up we are in a world we share with others, for as Heraclitus already said: 'The waking have one world in common. Sleepers meanwhile turn aside, each into a darkness of his own.'[2]

'Get up', says Christ to the benumbed disciples, 'and let us be going'. So let us also go with eager attentiveness out into every new day. We are expected.

VI

The Living Power of Hope

'May the God of hope fill you with all joy and peace in believing, so that by the power of the Holy Spirit you may abound in hope', writes Paul to the congregation in Rome (Rom. 15.13).

This is unique. Nowhere else in the world of the religions is God associated with human hope for the future. God is the one who is Eternally Present, the deity is the Wholly Other, what is divine is Timelessly Eternal: all that is common coin. God is 'above us' as the Almighty, or God is 'within us' as the ground of our being: that is familiar. But a God of hope, who is in front of us, and goes ahead of us in history? That is something new. We can find this only in the message of the Bible. This is the God of Israel's Exodus, who moves at the head of his people in the pillar of cloud by day and the pillar of fire by night. This is the God of Christ's resurrection, who leads those who are his to eternal life in the fire and tempest of the Holy Spirit. This God will 'dwell' among his people in 'the promised land'; this God will 'dwell' among human beings when all things are newly created in their truth, as the book of Revelation says (21.3). So God comes to meet men and women out of his future, and in their history reveals to them new, open horizons, which entice them to set forth into the unknown and invite them to the beginning of the new.

Christianity is wholly and entirely confident hope, a stretching out to what is ahead, and a readiness for a fresh start.[1] *Future* is not just something or other to do with Christianity. It is the essential element of the faith which is specifically Christian: the keynote of all its hymns, the dawn colouring of the new day in which everything is bathed. For faith is Christian faith when it is *Easter* faith. Faith means living in the presence of the risen

Christ, and stretching out to the coming kingdom of God. It is in the creative expectation of Christ's coming that our everyday experiences of life take place. We wait and hasten, we hope and endure, we pray and watch, we are both patient and curious. That makes the Christian life exciting and alive. The faith that 'another world is possible' makes Christians enduringly capable of future.

The Reasonableness of Hope

But how can we talk about a future which isn't yet there, and tell about events which no one has yet seen? Is this just wishful thinking? Are these nightmares or speculations which no one can check?

But the Christian hope doesn't talk about the future *per se* and all by itself, as an empty end towards which possible changes steer. It starts from a particular historical reality, and announces the future of that reality, its power over the future, and its consummation. The Christian doctrine of hope talks about *Jesus Christ and his future*. It is only in his name that hope is Christian. It is based on the remembrance of the coming, the death and the resurrection of Christ, and proclaims the coming of the One who is risen. Consequently for every Christian doctrine of hope, the justification of all expectations of the future in the person and history of Christ is the touchstone of all the utopian and apocalyptic spirits. Christian hope is based once and for all on the remembrance of Christ.

But the remembrance of Christ, for its part, throws open the wide horizons of the Christian hope. If the crucified Christ, on the foundation of his resurrection, has a future with God, then this means, conversely, that everything that is said about Christ says not only who he was and who he is, but must also say who he will be. With the familiar titles we give to Christ – Son of God, Son of man, Lord, Saviour, Redeemer – we are not merely expressing what he means for us; we are also saying what we expect of him. All the titles given to Christ are statements of hope. By announcing in the mode of promise his coming into this world, they draw believers into the expectation of his future. But in the promises of the gospel and the awakened hope of believers, his coming already acts, conversely, on the present, and makes believers ready to open themselves for his future.

At this point I must clarify an understandable misconception: according to the Apostles' Creed, it would seem as if since the ascension Christ has disappeared from the earth, is now sitting at a particular place in heaven, and is waiting for a time when he will all at once 'come again' to judge the living and the dead. That is the picture behind the saying about Christ's 'coming again'. But the phrase is misleading. Christ's hoped-for parousia – 'maranatha, come Lord Jesus' (Rev. 22.20) – is translated into Latin as *adventus Christi*, and that means his 'coming' in the sense of something coming to meet us out of the future (as we speak of a 'coming' event). If we talk about 'the second coming' of Christ, the present is empty, and all that is left to us is to wait for some far-off, final Judgement. But if we talk about 'Christ's coming', then he is already in the process of coming, and in the power of hope we open ourselves today with all our senses for the experiences of his arrival. By arrival we mean a future which is already present, yet without ceasing to be future. 'Jesus is in the process of coming'.[2]

Propositions count as true if they correspond to the reality which can be checked. But hope's assertions of promise often enough stand in contradiction to the reality of present experience. These assertions are not the outcome of past experiences they are an invitation to new ones. Their aim is not to illuminate the reality that already exists; they want to explore the possibilities ahead. Unlike every other perception of reality, they do not aim to be reality's train-bearers; they want to run ahead with the torch. 'The owl of Minerva' – the bird of wisdom – begins its flight only when night is falling. It is when a form of life has become old and finished that the hour of perception strikes.[3] But this doesn't make life young again. The bird of hope is different: it is like the lark which ascends at dawn, proclaiming the new day. Then the hour that strikes is the hour to wake up.

The present and the future, experience and hope, initially clash in Christian faith. Between them is the remembrance of Christ crucified by the powers of this world. It is only beyond the cross that we can see the first daybreak colours of God's new world.

This means that Christian hope is a 'hope against hope', or a hope where there is nothing else left to hope for. Calvin is rightly called the theologian of hope among the Reformers, and he put it like this:

> To us is promised eternal life – but to us, the dead. We are preached a blessed resurrection – but in the meantime we are surrounded by corruption. We are called just – and yet what dwells in us is sin. We hear of inexpressible blessedness – but in the meantime we are bowed down under unending misery. We are promised a superfluity of all good things – yet we are rich only in hunger and thirst. What would become of us if we did not obstinately cling to hope, and if our minds did not hasten along the paths lit up for us by God's Word and Spirit right through the darkness, beyond this world?
>
> (on Heb. 11.1)[4]

In these contradictions hope must prove its consoling and its resisting power. It is consoling to withstand and to stay the course in the expectation that 'He who endures to the end will be saved'. It is encouraging not to have to capitulate before the unalterability of conditions and not to give way to sadness, but to remain upright in protest. People who accept the darkness of their lives resist the light of God which drives out the night. Through the power of hope, we don't give up, and don't give ourselves up; we remain unreconciled and unaccepting in an unjust and deadly world.

Through the power of hope for the coming of God, the oppressed tell stories that run counter to the course of this world from which they suffer. There are the resurrection stories which the prophet Ezekiel tells to the despondent people (Ezek. 37): on the one side the fields of the dead, with the dried up bones of the people – on the other the living breath of God which awakens them and brings them to life. There are the apocalyptic images which we find in the book of Revelation about the fall of 'the great Whore of Babylon' – the symbol for Rome, which at that time was persecuting the Christians, and putting many of them to death. The image of 'the heavenly Jerusalem' in which God will finally dwell among human beings is the counter-image to imperial Rome, which down to the present day claims the name of 'the eternal city'. Even the title of Kyrios – Lord – for the crucified Jesus is a counter-title aimed at the Roman Caesar, who gave himself the same title, lord of the world. *Aut Christus, aut Caesar* – either Christ or Caesar: the Christian martyrs took the point, and refused to conform to the emperor cult, so as not to fall into the hands of lies and demons. In this sense the Christian hope's proclamation of God is *subversive* talk of God. Other lords and powers rule over us, but in you alone do we hope (Isa. 26.13).

In our respectable and conformist Christianity this subversive talk about God has become strange and alien. We don't understand the book of Revelation because we don't understand the martyrs. But Christians living under persecution, and Christians who are resisting injustice and violence, understand its language very well, for the language is their own.

Yet this spirit of resistance in hope for the coming of Christ and his kingdom is only the one side. We cannot always live merely in contradiction. Theoretically speaking, nothing positive comes simply out of the negation of the negative. We counter a world of injustice and violence either through mysticism or through active change. 'Ascetic Christianity called the world evil *and left it.* Humanity is waiting for a revolutionary Christianity which will call the world evil *and change it*', declared Walter Rauschenbusch.[5] That was the meaning of his 'social gospel' movement in America. The liberation theologians in Latin America followed him. But before we can change and improve this evil world we must change and improve ourselves. This happens when we turn about, and look to the future. In trust in God's coming, we open ourselves for his life-giving Spirit and experience the healing and liberating forces of that Spirit. These forces are not miraculous supernatural powers from heaven; as the Epistle to the Hebrews says (6.5), they are 'the powers of the age to come'. They come out of the promised future of Christ into our present and fill us with new vitality.

In the community of Christ we experience foretastes and anticipations of God's coming kingdom. To put it theoretically: hope lives from the anticipation of the positive and therefore sees itself as the negation of the negative. The two things belong together.

If in the present we can experience the kingdom of God in healings of mind, soul and body, then we can also do something for the kingdom of God. The kingdom of God has become Jesus' own affair. Through him it is already 'at hand', as the gospel says. In community with him, those who follow him in his messianic mission become co-workers for the kingdom. In Matt. 10.7f. the disciples are told: 'Preach, saying "the kingdom of heaven is at hand." Heal the sick, raise the dead, cleanse lepers, cast out demons', the very things which are said about Jesus himself in Matt. 11.4–5. So in Jesus' sense the kingdom is not just God's affair; it is ours as well. Through Jesus it has come so close to us that we don't just have to wait for it. We can already 'seek' it and its righteousness. It comes to us in such a way that we are to make it the goal of what we do in the world. How is this possible?

There are conditions in history which are in obvious contradiction to the kingdom of God and his righteousness and these we have to fight against. But there are also conditions which are in accord with the kingdom of God, and these we have to promote and, if we can, bring them into being. We shall then have *parables* of the coming kingdom now, in the present, and shall already anticipate today what will come about on the day of God. We shall already, here and now, let something of the healing and new creation of all things be seen which we expect in the future.[6] We can call this an action in *creative expectation*, just as during Advent we prepare for Christmas and, with the children, live in expectation of the feast: the time of Christian life is the season of Advent.

In the nineteenth century diaconal work and mission in Germany was called 'kingdom of God work'. Johann Hinrich Wichern's 'Rauhe Haus' in Hamburg, Gustav Wener's cooperative brotherhood in Reutlingen, Bodelschwingh's homes for the disabled in Bethel are examples in Germany. But we could name Elizabeth Fry's work for better prison conditions in England, Lord Shaftesbury's fight for factory legislation, the efforts of the abolitionists in America, Kagawa's social work in the slums of Tokyo; and much more. At that time work for the kingdom of God led beyond the frontiers of the Church out into society. Something similar took place in the peace movement in Germany, and in the movement for liberation in Latin America: from the Church to the kingdom of God in the world. But whether inside the Church or outside it, the place is the important thing, and that place is *this earth*. Seek first the kingdom of God on this earth. Christ won't just come to meet us out of heaven, but out of the earth too.

The Sin of Despair

If the Christian faith is dependent on the power of hope for its life and if reason is dependent on hope for its attentiveness, then without hope faith crumbles, and reason becomes cynical and unreasonable. 'Sin' doesn't mean some moral error; it means separation from God and from the life which God gives. True, we are told that the original sin was arrogance – that human beings wanted to be like God. But that is only half the truth. The other half is the resignation, which is much more widespread, the dejection which leads to inertia, the despondency which infects everything living with the germs of decay. The temptation today is not so much that human beings want to play God. It is much more that they no longer have confidence in the humanity which God expects of them. It is the fearfulness fed by lack of faith which leads to capitulation before the power of evil.

God has exalted human beings and opened to them a vista into what is wide and free, but human beings hang back and say no. God promises the new creation of all things, but human beings behave as if everything remains as it was. That is the separation from God and from life. It isn't the evil which human beings do that condemns them; it is rather the good that they fail to do – not only their great misdeeds, but their many small neglects. 'It is not so much sin which plunges us into disaster; it is rather our despair', said the Church Father John Chrysostom. And it is because of that that ever since the middle ages the list of the seven deadly sins has always begun with *accidia*, despondency. *Tristesse* is the sin against the Spirit of life from which all the other vices follow.

There are two forms of hopelessness. The one is arrogance or presumption (*praesumptio*). The other is despair, the obliteration of every hope (*desperatio*). In presumption we take the fulfilment of hope into our own hands, and no longer hope for God. In despair we doubt that there can ever be fulfilment, and destroy hope in ourselves. All despair presupposes hope. The pain of despair lies in the fact that hope exists, but that there appears to be no way for the hope to be fulfilled. Where hope for life is frustrated in every respect, the hope turns against the hoper and eats into him. 'I looked for work everywhere and was always turned down. Then I got to the point when nothing more mattered', said a young burglar in Berlin. When there is no longer any prospect of meaningful life, people turn to meaningless violence: 'Destroy whatever you can destroy.' When hope dies, the killing begins. Hopelessness and brutality are just two sides of the same sad coin.

Despair need not display only this distorted face of violence. It can also be the mere silent absence of any meaning, prospect and hope. *Bonjour tristesse!* All that is left is then ironic resignation. We have run through everything life has to offer and found nothing. The result is ennui, the boredom with life we can see among the rich and the beautiful people in this world. All that is left is a *taedium vitae,* an empty life of include-me-out. This is the so-called fun society of the western world. 'I want to have a good time', people say, and amuse themselves to death because their life is hollow and barren. The rest is diversion in the waiting room of death. In the soul of Europe we can see the burnt-out crater landscapes of quenched hopes. We can smell the odour of corruption of passions now dead. The cultural nihilism and the nihilistic indifference toward the mass murders in the world put their stamp on the twentieth century. That was so in big things, and in little ones too. 'It is not the crime on the streets which is the really evil thing', said a friend to me in New York after a daylight mugging. 'It is our indifference to them.'

Yet these different forms of despair cannot prevail against the creative power of hope, for they are only the symptoms of hope's decline. They spread only where hope withdraws and capitulates. When Christianity is no longer prepared to take public responsibility for the hope which God has placed in it, these petrifications and corruptions of life in society are the result. 'Always be prepared to make a defence for the hope that is in you,' we are told in 1 Peter 3.15. What hope is that? It is the hope of resurrection (Acts 23.6), and it already leads to a revolt against the powers of destruction here and now.

If we only had before us what we can see, then we should come to terms, whether cheerfully or reluctantly, with things as they are. But the fact that we do not come to terms with them – that between us and reality there is no harmony, either pleasurable or tedious, is due to the inextinguishable hope for the fullness of life. It keeps us unreconciled until God's great day. It keeps us on the move along the paths ahead. It fills us with that openness to the world which can never find fulfilment through anything except eternal life in the coming kingdom of God.

PART THREE

O BEGINNING
WITHOUT ENDING . . .

❧·❧

'The people's hope is the last to die.' I heard this proverb for the first time many years ago in Brazil. It came up again in August 2002, when the men and women living on the Elbe and Mulde fought for their homes, sometimes successfully, sometimes in vain, against the greatest flood Germany had known in living memory. 'Hope is the last to die', even if there is hardly any prospect of success and even if many lose heart and give up. The person who clings to hope resists to the end. If we give this brave proverb a positive turn, it has to run: hope survives everything, the floods and the broken dykes, the successes and the failures, the over-confidence and the despair; for everything that lives, lives from hope. So hope also helps us to survive the disappointments and devastations in our lives, literally to sur-vive – to live above them. *Dum spiro, spero* – as long as I breathe I hope, says another proverb. The breath of my soul is hope for life, the fulfilled life. As long as I breathe I hope, and the reverse is equally true: as long as I hope, I breathe in and breathe out these powers and energies for living.

If the vital power of hope is so much lauded in the proverbs of the different peoples, can't this power reach out beyond death as well? Shall we perhaps be immortal in hope, because what we hope for survives even our deaths? It is a hope which the poets have often expressed.[1] Tennyson was one of them. In his great elegy for his dead friend, *In Memoriam,* he writes:

Thou madest man, he knows not why,
He thinks he was not made to die;
And thou hast made him: thou art just.

But for the poet this is merely a thought, a possibility, a per-haps. In faith in the Christ risen from death, the 'perhaps' becomes a certainty. If our life ends in nothing but our dying, and in eternal death, then in our experience of life too farewells will take precedence over all the new beginnings, since everything we experience is, in the end, transitory, and passes away. But if Christ's farewell in his death has become the new, eternal beginning in his resurrection, then in our end we too shall find our new, eternal beginning. In the rebirth to a living hope, we already, here and now, come close to the primal force and wellspring of life. Will this primal force of life also be the power of resurrection which we approach in death? It is true that our lives end in death, but our deaths end in the raising to eternal life: that is then truer still. So death is the end, but not the last of all. Something else will come.

In the third part of this book I shall be looking at ideas about the world beyond in the light of the question: *is there a life after death?* I shall consider the practical consequences of these ideas under the heading: *'grieving and consoling'*. That leads of itself to the question about a *community between the living and the dead*. This will bring us to the weighty question: what do we expect or wait for? And what awaits us? Here I shall take up the common notion about the *Last Judgement*, Christianizing it fundamentally by integrating it into the other idea about the end, which is 'the restoration of all things'. Last of all, picking up the two key terms in the creeds, I shall try to elicit what *eternal life* and *'the life of the world to come'* can be.

The heading 'O Beginning without Ending' comes from an old German hymn by Johann Rist (1607–67), which defines eternity paradoxically as a 'time without time'.[2] A beginning that has no end, and a time without time, are phrases that make us sit up and pay attention: in English phraseology, 'world without end' and 'life everlasting'. It is this to which we shall now turn in the third part of the book.

VII

Is There a Life After Death?

Is Death the Finish?

What is left of our lives when we die? Why do we ask? What are we asking about? We ask questions like this when we stop still in the flux of time and look for something that can sustain us.

Where are the dead? We ask about their future when we bury those we love and mourn the people who were our life's happiness; for when they die, our love for life dies too. So where are we going? Do we expect, await anything? And what awaits us?

What is left? Is anything left at all? Of course this question overwhelms us when we feel the cold breath of death, either our own death or the death of the people we love. Death seems final: past – gone – nevermore.

But this is not just the question about death at the end of a lifetime. The question is always with us already as the question about time, for 'our years are soon gone, and we fly away', as Psalm 90 says. We cannot hold fast to a single instant, however much we long to say 'O tarry a while, thou art so fair'. For we ourselves cannot tarry. The lived moment passes, and we pass away in a moment. Nothing remains, for what has once become past can never be brought back. The future for which we hope and for which we labour will one day, if it comes about, become our present, and our expectations will then become the experiences we once longed for. But every present passes away, and what is past never returns. Expectations become experiences, and experiences become memories, and remembering will ultimately become the great forgetting we call death. So does nothing await us – or even Nothingness?

Something within us rebels against this, protesting: is that all life has to offer?

If people discover no positive answer, they find it easy to hand back their ticket to this life. In Norway and Switzerland, the richest countries in Europe, the suicide rate among young people is the highest of all. 'We are living in paradise and are stuck in hell', Norwegian students told me. There are external sufferings which make life unacceptable – to be unwanted, to be un-employed, to be ill. And there are inward sufferings which make it difficult to affirm life inspite of all its senselessness. Wolf Biermann cried out in his song the deficit so many people feel:

> That surely can't have been all,
> that little bit of Sunday and children's voices.
> It's surely got to lead somewhere!
>   . . .
> That surely can't have been all.
> There has to be something ahead –
> No, we have to get life into life, that's it.[1]

But what life is it, that we have to get into this life? And where is the 'somewhere' it must lead to? What is the 'something ahead'?

When we ask about a life *after* death, we are always asking at the same time about a meaningful, liveable and loved life *before* death.

What could a life after death mean for us if before death there cannot be a fulfilled life which we can affirm?

In the first part of this chapter we shall discuss various religious and philosophical ideas about immortality, looking at them under the heading: 'what is left of life?'

In the second section we shall discuss various ideas about eternal life, looking at them under the heading: 'where are the dead?'

Our question is certainly: is there a life after death? But what we know about that life doesn't belong to the sphere of the scientific knowledge we have at our disposal about circum-stances that can be experienced and facts that can be proved. It belongs to another sphere, the sphere of the knowledge that sustains existence, which gives confidence in life and comfort in dying. We shall examine ideas in this sector from the aspect of their consequences for this life here, and for our dealings with death – our own death and the death of other people – and for our community with the dead.

What Is Left of Life? Are We Mortal or Immortal?

We are all familiar with very old religious ideas or images about the human being's immortal soul, which after death leaves the body behind and returns to its eternal home in a heaven beyond the earth. The ancient Egyptians depicted the soul as a bird with the human face of the dead person. In the pictures painted by children in the Theresienstadt concentration camp, Elisabeth Kübler-Ross discovered especially many pictures of butterflies: the poor caterpillar breaks out of its chrysalis and flies away, a beautiful butterfly, out into the wide world. Medieval pictures show the soul as a tiny human being with angel's wings entering the body before birth, so that after the person's death it can fly away and return to heaven. In Germany, death notices are often headed by a famous verse of Eichendorff's:

And my soul spread wide her wings,
flew through the silent land
as if she flew towards home.

It is a beautiful picture, even if the last line, with its 'as if', embodies romantic insubstantiality. Yet every prisoner in his cell and every invalid on his sick bed knows the longing awakened by the free flight of a bird, the yearning for 'the broad place where there is no cramping'.

But what do we mean when we talk about our immortal soul? Do we mean the immortality of the unlived life, or the immortality of the lived life?

According to our philosophical tradition, which began with Plato, the human soul is in substance essentially immortal.[2] Death does not kill it, but merely separates the immortal soul from the mortal body, which then lies there a lifeless corpse. The body's death may be something to be lamented by everyone who loved it, with its senses and passions. But for the soul, death is what Dietrich Bonhoeffer called the greatest feast day on the way to freedom. Because it is immortal, in this mortal body it was merely a guest on a beautiful planet, or was as if imprisoned.

We now have to ask: why should the soul in particular be immortal, while everything else about us is mortal? The answer is a simple one, even if it is not a matter of common knowledge. The soul cannot die because it has never been born. Because it was there before the child's birth, it will still be there after the person has died, full of years. The soul's 'life after death' is also its 'life before birth', for its 'eternal life' is beyond the birth and death of this life. But if the soul has never been born and never dies, it has nothing in common with the bodily, sensory world of this life, which is both born and mortal. It is in its substance immutable, always the same, insusceptible to suffering and hence incapable of happiness as well. In the sense of what we call lived life and livingness, it is un-living. We might put the matter in a nutshell and say that the idea of an immortal soul doesn't mean the immortality of the life lived here; it means the immortality of the life eternally unlived. But if that is true, then this doctrine about the immortal soul fails to provide us with an answer to the question: what will be left of this life?

Yet the consciousness of 'possessing' an immortal soul contributes to equanimity in the changes and chances of life, and to indifference towards life and death. The self-transcendence that sets one above things, and the self-irony that prevents one from taking oneself too seriously, let alone with deadly seriousness: these are the virtues of the people supported by this belief. We find this attitude not just in the philosophy of the Greek Stoa but in the Indian *Bhagavad-Gita* too:

> Never is it born nor dies; never did it come to be nor will it ever come to be again: unborn, everlasting . . .
> For wise men there are, the same in pleasure as in pain, whom these (contacts) leave undaunted: such are conformed to immortality . . .
> The man who puts away all desires and roams around from longing freed, who does not think 'This I am', or 'This is mine', draws near to peace.[3]

Perhaps there were closer links between Greece and India than we know of.

But when we talk about the soul today do we really mean these characteristics of inward insusceptibility? German talks about a 'beseelten Leben' – an ensouled life, meaning a life that is completely and wholly alive: open, able to be happy, able to suffer, a life full of love. If we say that a mother is the life and soul of her family, we don't mean that she is the unmoved member of the family; we mean that she holds her family together through her love, and makes it a living entity.

Consequently I should like to understand the soul in a different way from Plato and say: human life is completely human when it is completely alive. But human livingness means being interested in life, participating, communicating oneself, and affirming one's own life and the life of other people. We call this interest in life, love for life. It expresses itself in life that is fully lived because it is life that is loved. Our 'soul' can always be found where we are entirely concentrated on something, are passionately interested, and by virtue of love do not hold our lives back but go out of ourselves and invest our lives. As long as you are concerned, you are present. But if we go out of ourselves in this way, we become capable of happiness, but capable of suffering too. It is love that lets us experience both the livingness of life and the deadliness of death. Yet how can we really give ourselves up to this life, with its conflicts, its happiness and its disappointments and pains, if what we expect of this love for life is nothing more than fleeting time and a death that is final? The really human problem is not the dualism of an immortal soul and a mortal body; it is the conflict between love and death.

Is there such a thing as immortality for this loved, ensouled and mortal life?

This apparent contradiction is resolved if we ascribe immortality not to a substance or some untouchable nucleus within us (such as the Platonic soul) but to the relationship of the whole person to the immortal God. Christian theology has worked on this transformation of the concept of the soul ever since its beginnings.[4] I may mention a number of different stages and aspects.

(a) Both the Old and the New Testaments attribute immortality to the divine Spirit which gives us and all earthly beings life (*ruach, pneuma*). 'Into thy hands I commit my spirit', prays the dying Jesus according to Luke (23.46), using the words of Ps. 31.6, the Jewish evening prayer. We find this echoed in Edward Caswell's translation of a Latin hymn:

> As Christ upon the cross in death reclined,
> Into his Father's hands his parting soul resigned,
> So now herself my soul would wholly give
> Into his sacred charge in whom all spirits live.[5]

According to biblical ideas, this Spirit who is the giver of life (*spiritus vivificans*) is a divine relationship from which life and the blessing of life emerge. What divine relationship? A relationship of love?

(b) Human beings have been created to be God's image on earth; that is to say, God puts himself in a relationship to these created beings of such a kind that they become the mirror, the reflection and the resonance of God himself. If God is God, God's relationship to his human image cannot be destroyed either through the contrariety of sin or through the death of human beings. Only God himself could dissolve the relationship he has entered into towards those he has created, if he were to 'repent' or be sorry for having made human beings, in the way that the story of Noah and the Flood relates. But as long as God sustains this relationship to human beings, their destiny to be the image of God remains, inalienable, indestructible. If this were not the case, the forces of time and death would be mightier than God. What emerges for human beings from this special loving relationship of God's to them is called 'life' or 'soul' or 'spirit'.

(c) This does not at all mean what we generally mean by our word 'spirit'. The Hebrew word *ruach* means vitality, the power of life. It fills the whole of a lived life, that is to say the whole history of our lives from birth to death – everything, that is, which we describe through a person's name.

> Thus says the Lord: Fear not, for I have redeemed you,
> I have called you by your name. You are mine.

So we say, with Isaiah 43.1, at sick beds or when we stand at the graveside. But then what do we mean by a person's name?

Surely not his or her bodiless soul or de-souled body! We mean the whole configuration of the person's life, in space and time, that person's whole biography. If the whole form this life takes, and this whole life history is called by name, then that means logically that within God's relationship to us our whole life is immortal. As mortal, transitory men and women we remain immortal and non-transitory in the immortal and non-transitory community with God himself. How ought we to understand this?

(d) The American process theology of A. N. Whitehead and Charles Hartshorne has given the name of 'objective immortality' to this endurance in the relationship with God.[6] God does not only act on everything; everything acts back upon God as well. Human beings are not merely created by God; they in their turn also make an impression on God. It is not only we who experience God; God also 'experiences' us, and the 'experience' which God has with us remains existent in God, even when we die. Our life is transitory in time, but in God we have an eternal presence. The history of our lives is fleeting, and we ourselves quickly forget it; but for God it is like a 'book of life' which remains eternally in God's memory in just the way God has experienced our lifetime.

This idea of an 'objective immortality' in God's eternity is not really in itself a comforting idea. Do we in fact want to have recalled to all eternity everything we have ever said, done and experienced? Moreover, according to the psalms in the Old Testament, God's memory is not a video of our lives, recorded in heaven and played through eternally; it is a compassionate, healing memory, which puts things right: 'Remember me according to your mercy' and 'remember not the sins of my youth'. It is the 'shining face' of God's love which looks at us, not the chilly lens of a monitor set up by some supervisory office for state security.

(e) The relationship of human beings to God out of which they come alive is also called 'dialogue immortality'. 'The one with whom God speaks, be it in wrath or be it in grace, that one is assuredly immortal', said Luther. Many Protestant and Catholic theologians maintain that men and women remain God's 'contact', even if they don't listen to him.[7] Even death cannot alter that. But if they do listen, then their whole life becomes a responding existence: they respond, and become responsible. If this is correct, then death is of course the limit of our lives, but it is not the limit of God's relationship to us. In the relationship of our lives, death is rather a gateway, a transformation on our side. The speaking, calling and finally redeeming relationship of God to us endures.

(f) Finally, in faith there is an experience in the fellowship of Christ which leads to a subjective immortality and to a positive hope for resurrection. That is the experience of being a child of God in the Spirit of God. 'Those who are led by the Spirit of God are the children of God', says Paul. As God's children we are the children of a king, and are of divine lineage. In the power of hope, we already participate here in the eternal life of God's future world. We already experience here that eternal life in the Spirit of the resurrection; we experience it as eternal livingness in love.

So – what is left of life?

We have two impressions. On the one hand there is nothing to which we can hold fast, not even ourselves. Everything passes away. We came naked into the world and naked we shall leave it. Death is the finish.

But on the other hand, nothing at all is lost. Everything remains in God.[8]

With God, we mortal beings are immortal, and our perishable life remains imperishably existent in God. We experience our life as temporal and mortal. But as God experiences it, our life is eternally immortal. Nothing is lost to God, not the moments of happiness, not the times of pain. 'All live to him' (Luke 20.38).

Where Are the Dead?

What sounds like a speculative question is not really speculative at all. Where do we truly experience death? At the end of my life I experience dying but I don't experience my own death, because on this earth I don't survive it. But in the case of the people I love, I experience their death when they die, for I have to survive their death, and have to mourn their loss, and go on living in spite of it. Life is good, but it is hard to be a survivor and harder still to be bereaved.

This means that we ourselves experience dying, but in other people we experience death. The poet Mascha Kaléko put it aptly in her poem 'Memento':

> I am not afraid of my own death,
> Only of the death of those near to me.
> How can I live when they are no longer there?
>
> . . .
>
> Remember: with our own death we merely die,
> but with the death of others we have to live.[9]

The question, where are the dead? is an important question personally, because it is the question about the community of the living with the dead, and for a life in the presence of the dead the answer is important.

I can remember what was for me a painfully embarrassing situation. Ernst Bloch had died. He lived in our neighbourhood, and I went over at once to talk to his wife. She came towards me and simply asked: 'Where is he now?' Bloch's body was still lying there. For the moment I wasn't able to find an adequate answer. But I have learnt that this 'where' question is important for those left behind, because without an answer they are unable to cling to their community with 'the beloved person', as Carola Bloch called her husband.

Let us now look at three ideas about the life of the dead, and then ask critically whether the love of the living for the dead is strengthened by them.

(a) The doctrine of purgatory is unknown in Protestant circles or among people outside the churches. In an oral exam, a Protestant theological student once answered my question about purgatory by saying that he supposed it was hell for the Catholics. The starting point for the development of the Church's idea about purgatory goes back to a declaration of Pope Benedict XII in 1336.[10] He rejected the idea that the dead are asleep until they are raised at the Last Judgement, and maintained that everyone is judged immediately after his or her personal death. The dead are confronted with the whole truth of the life they have lived, in the light of the way it is seen by God. They will know as they are known, because they are standing before their eternal judge. In the face of death many people have experienced something like this. Their whole lives pass before them in a single flash. If someone dies in faith in Christ, their sins are forgiven, but the consequences of the sins are still there, because they have not yet been expiated through the suffering of temporal punishments. Just as life before death is already a continual repentance, life after death is continued as a process of purification and refining. That is purgatory. It has nothing to do with hell. On the contrary, it is the way to heaven. To put it simply, in death the believing soul experiences the presence of God as light and fire. The light of eternal love draws it to God; the fire of eternal love burns up everything which is in contradiction to God and which cuts the soul off from God. Many people who have stood at the threshold of death tell of visions of this kind, visions of light and fire. The fundamental idea behind the doctrine of purgatory is to be found in Christ's promise that 'the pure in heart shall see God'. Consequently the purification of the heart must be continued until the blissful contemplation of God, the beatific vision, can take place.

In the religious world of ideas, heaven and hell are final stages, one of them without desire, the other without hope. But the idea of purgatory allows God's history with men and women to continue beyond their deaths. It opens up a hopeful path after death. That is why in Dante's *Divine Comedy* (1319) over the gateway to purgatory stand the words 'Beloved son, let your hopes rise', whereas the gateway to hell is headed 'Abandon hope all ye who enter here'. In Dante, purgatory lies on a mountain of purification, with seven stages, which lead from earth to heaven.

Can the living do anything for the souls in purgatory? 'We can efficaciously help the dead', says a Catholic tenet. For in Christ the living and the dead form a great communion. It is an 'expiatory community'. So the person who is granted an indulgence for sins has the right to ask God to credit the remission of his own punishment to the dead, so that their period in purgatory may be shortened. But Masses for the dead provide the most efficacious help.

The Protestant criticism of purgatory is well known. After all, the Reformation began with Luther's criticism of Tetzel's traffic in indulgences, which we are told was accompanied by the slogan: 'As soon as the money chinks in the box, out of purgatory the soul hops.' Luther then also criticized the 'fairground trafficking in purgatorial Masses'[11] and Calvin even called purgatory 'a pernicious invention of Satan'.

Both Luther and Calvin preached that on the cross Christ did enough for our sins once and for all, so that the souls of the dead require no other 'satisfaction'; they do not have to win blessedness by undergoing punishment, and the dying no longer have to torment themselves with feelings of guilt and fears of judgement. But in saying this the Reformers were merely criticizing the notion of expiation, and only the 'expiatory community' of the living and the dead. They were not criticizing the idea that God's history with human beings continues after their death. Nor did they condemn the lasting community of the living and the dead in Christ.

(b) Another idea which we find in Luther and among modern Catholic theologians is the doctrine of the soul's sleep, or the resurrection at death.[12] Luther imagined the state of the dead as a deep, dreamless 'sleep', removed from time and space, without consciousness and without feeling. In this idea he thought not so much from here to there as from there to here: when the dead are raised by Christ at 'the Last Day', they know neither how long they have slept nor where they have been. We shall rise 'suddenly', not knowing how we entered into death, and how we have come through it. 'As soon as thy eyes have closed shalt thou be woken, a thousand years shall be as if thou hadst slept but a little half hour. Just as at night we hear the clock strike and know not how long we have slept, so too, and how much more, are in death a thousand years soon past. Before a man should turn round, he is already a fair angel.' The theological justification runs as follows: 'Because before God's face time is not counted, a thousand years before him must be as if it were but a single day. Hence the first man Adam is as close to him as will be the last to be born before the Final Day. For God seeth time, not according to its length but athwart it, transversely. Before God all hath happened at once.'

When Luther calls death a sleep, that is not a way of disguising the harsh fact of death. His purpose is to maintain that death has lost its power over human beings, and that it is not the last thing that we have to expect. The presupposition of both these assertions is Christ's resurrection with the dead, for with that, death relinquished its power to Christ. Death still has its character or 'form', as Luther puts it, but no longer its 'power'.

How long does the 'sleep of souls' or 'death's dark night' last? Luther does not answer by projecting the time of the living on to the continuing existence of souls after death. Instead he finds ways of expressing God's time: 'suddenly', 'in the twinkling of an eye'. The Last Day is the Day of the Lord, and consequently it is not just the last day in the calendar but the day of days. God's time is the time of the eternal present. How long will it be from the hour of our own death until the dead are raised into the eternal kingdom? Just 'an instant'. Where are the dead now, in terms of our time? They are already in the world of the resurrection. 'Today', said Christ to the man dying beside him on the cross: 'Today' – not in three days – not at the Last Day – but 'Today you will be with me in paradise' (Luke 23.43).

Karl Rahner and other Catholic theologians have taken up this idea about 'the resurrection at death'. The ecumenical 'Book of Belief' (*Das Glaubensbuch*) of 1973 says: 'The individual resurrection from the dead takes place at and with death'. Unfortunately, in 1979 Joseph Ratzinger, in his first declaration as cardinal, had these ideas rejected by the Congregation for the Doctrine of the Faith, because they make indulgences and Masses for the dead superfluous, and are therefore contrary to the Church's practice.

(c) That brings us to a question which is much discussed today: the question of possible reincarnations. Do we live on earth only once, or are we reborn in many different forms?[13]

Although a soul which cannot die is not born either, the idea of an immortal soul has often been linked from time immemorial with ideas about the transmigration of souls and reincarnation in new forms of life. Everything living comes into being and passes away. Why shouldn't it come into being afresh? If we cease to look at our own little lives, and contemplate the great warp and weft of life in human communities, and the community in life of all the living, then the notion of an eternal return is quite normal, and the idea of the unique originality of a single life is really something special. Plato and Plotinus, Lessing and Goethe were attracted by the idea of reincarnation. The New Age movement has taken it up. Let us now compare the old and new doctrine of reincarnation with the biblical (i.e., Jewish and Christian) views of life and death.

1. Every doctrine of reincarnation sets the individual life in the wider community of generations and of all the living. Everything is related to everything else. Don't kill an animal, the soul of your mother could be within it! Do no wrong to any living thing, because you could be that living thing yourself in the next life! If the souls of human beings, animals and plants are seen in the great cohesion of the world soul, then we are all living together in an ensouled cosmos.

For the Abrahamic religions, on the other hand, the uniqueness of the human person and the 'once-and-for-all' character of the individual life goes hand in hand with the counterpart of a personal God. Human beings are not just part of nature, as the Earth Charter of the United Nations says. They are also the image of the invisible God. In this relationship to God they are elevated above the cohesions of nature. Before God, every human person is an original, not a replica. The consequence is the high regard for the individuality of every life, and an awareness and appreciation of the uniqueness of the lived moment.

From the biblical standpoint, the doctrines of reincarnation are faced with the question of whether their ideas do not considerably reduce the number of existing souls. Doesn't the claim to have lived several times, or to be reborn again and again, mean an outrageous ousting of other persons from their own lives? I remember a film in which a Tibetan Lama dies, and the monks look for the person in whom his soul has been reborn. They find this reborn soul in a little Chinese boy. They take him with them, and make of him the reincarnation of the dead Lama. The boy can no longer live his own life, for he is no longer himself.

From the standpoint of the doctrines of reincarnation, the Abrahamic religions face the question of whether personal stress on the individual over and above the cohesions of nature does not destroy the community of life on earth, and whether it is not responsible for the ecological catastrophes of the modern world.

That brings us to the synthesis: as persons before God, human beings are part of nature, and as part of nature they are persons before God. Their unique character as the image of God does not isolate them from nature; it merely describes their special task within nature. Persons are not individuals; they are beings in community, and they live in community with one another, in the community of the generations, and within the community of creation. It is not merely possible to mediate fruitfully to each other the Western understanding of the person and the Eastern understanding of nature. This mediation is vitally necessary.

The critical questions are to be found at a totally different point.

2. Every doctrine of reincarnation is faced with the question whether the soul's identity is to be preserved in the transformation of the forms its life takes.[14] If I am born again as a human being, I must be able to keep the human identity of my soul. If I am reborn as an animal, or if I once died as a tree, this identity cannot be preserved. It passes away together with the human form my life took. If I have the impression that 'I have been here before', I must be able to recognize myself in that past form of life. My 'I', my 'self', cannot be mortal. But if my 'I' is part of this life, then I cannot recognize myself again, however often I am reborn. According to ancient Indian teaching, moreover, the soul does not really migrate. It is true that the *Bhagavad-Gita* says:

> As a man casts off his worn-out clothes
> and takes on other new ones,
> so does the embodied [self] cast off
> its worn-out bodies and enters other new ones.[15]

But if the soul is without individuality, then it is not a determining subject that migrates or casts off its clothes either. So in Buddhism a further idea was developed, about a 'transmigration of souls without a soul'.

> Is the one who is born again
> the same as the one who departs or different?
> Neither the same nor another:
> one appearance emerges, another disappears,
> yet they all range themselves to each other without
>   interruption.

In this way the final version of the consciousness is attained neither as the same person nor as another.
Life is without a beginning and without an end.

That is a typically Asiatic neither-nor answer to a typically Western either-or question.

3. According to ancient Indian doctrine, reincarnations belong to the meaningless wheel of rebirth, and as karma are the requital for the good and evil deeds in a former life. Rebirths are, so to speak, the materialized consequences of guilt. According to Western Spiritism and New Age, however, they are part of the evolutionary principle of the modern world. What is karma? The ancient karma doctrine maintains an inexorable and inescapable cohesion between act and destiny: 'The one who steals corn will become a rat', and 'as a man sows, so he will reap.' This coherence cannot be broken by any power in the world, or by any God.

But in its Western interpretation, reincarnation is supposed to give us a second chance, so that we can do better next time. This is what Elisabeth Kübler-Ross thinks. 'We climb higher and higher up the ladder of progress until the stage of perfection is reached', taught the spiritist Alan Kardec. So there is a contradiction between the Eastern and the Western judgement of reincarnation; it is either a punishment or a chance.

The biblical religions are also aware of a karma which spans the generations: 'The fathers have eaten sour grapes, and the children's teeth are set on edge.' That is generally accepted wisdom. 'He who sows the wind will reap the whirlwind.' But what is special and new in the biblical traditions is the principle of grace, which breaks the link between act and destiny, and sets this law aside: 'His mercies are new every morning.' The One 'who forgives all your iniquity, and heals all your diseases' is himself the power of life which breaks through karma and fate, replacing an endless requital by the new beginning.

This means, finally, that the cosmic law of karma can no longer be used to explain disabilities, sicknesses or sufferings in this present life, putting them down to the guilt of those who have gone before us. What karmic guilt are the dead of Auschwitz supposed to have expiated? What karmic retaliation are the dead of Hiroshima supposed to have suffered? A handicapped child . . .?

The Future of the Life Cut Short and Spoiled

Much in our life remains unfinished. We started something but never completed it. We tried to map out a plan for our life, but the plan was spoiled. Life was promised us, and the promise wasn't kept. How can a life here ever be 'finished' or count as being 'successful'?

What awaits us? However we may think of eternal death or eternal life, it cannot surely be the eternalization of our unsuccessful beginnings or failed attempts at life. It is impressions of this kind which makes us think further about an ongoing history on God's part with the lives we have lived, because they make us feel that the dead have not yet come to rest. The impression remains that, whether as purgatory or reincarnation, I shall come back again to this life, so as to put right what went wrong, to bring to an end what was once begun, to pick up what was neglected, to pay the debts and heal the pains, and to complete the uncompleted.

But it is not just the caesuras in our own biographies which make us ask about a life after death. I am thinking about the life of those who were unable to live and were not permitted to live: the beloved child who died at birth, the little boy run over when he was four, the 16-year-old friend torn to pieces at your side by the bomb which left you unscathed – and the countless people raped, murdered or 'liquidated'. Of course their fate can have great meaning for other people, but where and how will their own lives be completed? Where and how will they find rest?

The idea that for these people their death is 'the finish' would plunge this whole world into absolute absurdity, for if their life had no meaning, has ours? The modern notion about a 'natural death' may be appropriate for the life-insured denizens of the affluent society, who can afford death in old age; but most people in the Third World die a premature, violent and by no means affirmed death, like the millions of young people in my generation who died in the Second World War. The idea that death is 'the eternalization of life as it has been lived' doesn't at all take in the people who were not able to live or were not permitted to do so. So mustn't we think the thought of an ongoing history of God's with lives that have been broken off and destroyed in this way, if we are to be able to affirm life in this world in spite of its destructions, and love life in spite of all its cruelties, and protect it against these cruelties and acts of inhumanity?

I believe that God will also complete the life which he has begun with a human being (Phil. 1.6). If God is God, even violent death cannot prevent him from doing so. So I believe that God's history with our lives will continue after our deaths, until the completion is reached in which a soul will find its wrongs redressed, and will find rest and happiness. According to ancient tradition this is not yet 'the kingdom of God', nor is it as yet 'the life of the world to come'; it is a kind of 'intermediate state' between the life that has died here and the life that will be eternal there. It is an intermediate state of this kind which is presupposed by the doctrine of purgatory and the doctrine of reincarnation; but the idea of a great divine Judgement is also a way of giving a name to something between our death and eternal life.

I do not believe in necessary expiations in some purgatory. I do not believe in a great, final, divine punitive Judgement either. For me, God's judgement means the final redressing of the wrong that has been committed and suffered, and the final raising up of those who are bowed down. That is why I imagine that intermediate state as a wide space for living in which the life which was cut short and destroyed here can develop freely. I imagine it as a new time for living in which God's history with a human being goes on, and arrives at completion. I imagine that in death we come very close to that well of life from which we already here and now draw strength to live and to affirm life, so that those who have been injured, broken and destroyed can live the life for which they were destined, for which they were born, and which was taken from them.

Consequently I do not believe either that we ought to compare that life after death with a sleep, as Luther did. I rather think with Calvin of a great 'wakefulness of the soul' after death, in which it 'perceives' its healing and its completion, and 'experiences' its rebirth to the eternal life of the world to come.[16] Those we call the dead are not lost. But they are not finally saved either. Together with us, who are still alive, they are sheltered and kept safe in the same hope, so that together with us they are on the way to God's future. They 'watch' with us, and we 'watch' with them. That is the community of hope shared by the dead with the living, and the living with the dead.

I think this, not for selfish reasons, neither for the sake of a personal completion, nor for the sake of a moral purification or refining. I think it for the sake of the justice which I believe is God's own concern and his first option.

VIII

Mourning and Consoling

Experiences of Life and Death Today

In the Caracalla baths in Rome, there is an old Roman mosaic which shows a dying man who, as he falls to the ground, points with his finger to the inscription below. We should expect the old saying: *memento mori*, 'remember that you must die'. But what is written there is *gnothi seauton*, 'know thyself'.[1] Taking up this reminder of the need for self-knowledge in the face of death, let us now ask about the spiritual dimensions of mourning and consoling.

All human life draws towards death. This fact is unalterable. It is the fact that we must die which distinguishes us from the immortal gods; the fact that we know it which distinguishes us from animals. What wisdom about life do we gain when we remember that we must die, and what foolishness when we forget that we are mortal?

Unlike other living things, human beings know in the prime of life, and even as children, that they are going to die. Death is not merely the medical fact that a life has ended. It is also the death of the whole person, and thus an event belonging to the whole of life. We take it into account in the whole way we live, consciously and unconsciously. We can repress the idea of our own death, and behave as if we were leading a life without death. We can make silent compacts with death, and promise ourselves certain years of life. We can live in a continual protest against death. We can accept it and integrate it into our awareness of life. Our attitudes to life and our plans for living always reflect our attitudes to death. What had some point in our lives, and what was pointless, then often becomes manifest when we die. That is true not only of the personal way we structure our living; it also applies to the culture in which we live. Every culture develops its own lifestyle, and with that lifestyle its own public awareness of death too.

As far as the personal structuring of life is concerned, the problem is not simply *life* and death; it is *love* and death. For life and death are not just biological facts. They are fundamental experiences which are bound up with each other. Life can be affirmed or denied. If it is affirmed and accepted, we talk about love for life, and joy in living. Only a life that is loved, accepted and affirmed can be a happy life. An unloved, rejected or denied life petrifies and dies. That is the experience of every new-born child. These are the very first experiences of life at all.

Through love we come alive, and make other people alive, but love also makes us vulnerable for disappointments and hurts, and ultimately for death. Love doesn't give us joy in life without the pain of death. If we want to avoid the pain, we reduce our capacity for happiness too. If we are overwhelmed by pain and grief, we often withdraw our interest in life, and become apathetic. The person who has seen too much blood shed, and too many dead bodies, can be as if numbed, and in the end completely indifferent to life and death. He couldn't care less, as we say. In a state like this, feeling and thinking petrify. Just as *rigor mortis* is a sign of death, human beings die a living death, spiritually speaking, if they grow hard and numb.

The correspondence between the readiness for happiness and the capacity for suffering moulds not only our personal lives but our public culture too. Social life is mainly shaped by rituals. Where in the public life of our society do we find the rituals for dying, death and mourning? The answer is plain: we hardly notice these things at all. When someone dies, it is seldom at home and in the circle of the family. It is much more frequently in hospital, and in the intensive care unit at that. Members of the family and friends of the dying person 'can't do anything more'. The doctors 'can't do anything more' either. So many people die alone, left to themselves. The modern activist culture finds its end when it comes to dying, death and mourning.

Burial grounds are no longer churchyards in the middle of villages. They are on the outskirts of town or city. Undertakers and 'funeral parlours' take over all responsibility, so that the family has nothing to worry about. Neighbours and friends shake hands silently with the mourners, because there is nothing more they can do. In public life, mourners no longer have any status. Women no longer wear black, and men no longer have black armbands on their coats. Before the First World War there were two large stores in London selling mourning clothes. In the 1920s they disappeared. 'Life must go on' seems to be the ultimate public consolation.

The dying and the grieving seem to excuse themselves: 'Please don't let me be in your way.' Modern society has no time for mourning, and no space, so it has no respect and no protection for mourners either. Death and mourning have been radically privatized and banished from public life, except for state ceremonies and state funerals for prominent statesmen. In Sweden, people are given one free day after a death in the family, though in Israel it is a whole week. The disruptions of public life which a death causes are generally swept aside as rapidly as possible. There seems to be a taboo about everything which has to do with death. In these sectors modern men and women are communication-disabled. It is only in the case of road accidents that we experience the death of other people directly and at first hand. But as quickly as the accident takes place, the dead are taken away and the wreckage is removed, for 'the traffic must be kept moving'.

And yet dying, death and mourning are present in modern civilization. They are present, just as everything else we suppress is still present, and unconsciously oppresses us. The various ways in which we repress death and mourning make modern men and women speechless, apathetic and infantile. The always somewhat forced 'fun' culture, and the pressurizing compulsion to *do* something, can be viewed as consequences of these public attempts at repression. We increasingly perceive events merely in the technical sense, and no longer in human terms. The modern inability to grieve is probably also grounded in the media culture of the modern world. We note what we see on the television screen, but it hardly touches us. We see the world through the mirror of the media and don't know whether they are giving us a reflection of the real world or not. The secondary experiences communicated through the media overlie our primary existential experiences. What is authentic and what isn't? We can no longer distinguish. So did the Gulf War really take place in Iraq, or only on the CNN channel?

But personal experience also helps us to repress the awareness of death. The modern world offers us countless opportunities for life and experience, but our lives are short. The unconscious fear of missing out on something, or of being done out of something, is a tremendous accelerator in the way we live – and it is not for nothing that the résumé we present on applying for a job is called a *curriculum vitae* – the 'race' of our lives. Everything about us is modernized faster and faster, and we hurry and rush from one place to another in order to experience something. We collect more and more experiences, and consume more and more rapidly without any apparent limitation of the speed. Fast food – fast life! But it is only the person who lives slowly who really experiences something of life. It is only if we digest what we experience that we have experienced something. It is only if we eat slowly that we enjoy what we eat. It is only if we can pause over an impression that we can absorb it. The unconscious fear of death hounds us through life, and life passes us by as we hurry past it. And yet we do not have to run after every possibility. One reality is of more value than a thousand possibilities.

Only Love Can Mourn

What is mourning, and how do we mourn? Is mourning the reverse side of love, and is its pain the mirror-writing of love's delight? The greater the love, the deeper the grief; the more unreserved the surrender, the more inconsolable the loss. Those who have given themselves utterly in love for someone else die themselves in the pains of grief, and are born again so that life can be given to them afresh, and so that they can again find the will to live. This is what personal experience and the experience of other people tell us. But if this is true we must take, or leave ourselves, just as much time for mourning as for love. It is only the grief which is accepted and suffered-through which restores the love for life after a death. People who shut themselves off from the mourning process or who cut it short will discover in themselves insurmountable depression and increasing apathy. They will lose contact with the reality of the people around and will be unable to find new courage for living. The person who mourns deeply has loved greatly. The person who cannot mourn has never loved. It is true that at the present time and in our present culture we are so conditioned that we want to have happiness without pain, and love without grief. We flee the grief and seek a painless happiness. What is on offer in modern society, culturally and medically, is designed to meet this personal wish. But if it is true that mourning is not the farewell to love but love's reverse side, then we can explore the mystery of mourning without fear, and surrender ourselves to mourning without being afraid of losing ourselves.

The process of mourning has for everyone a very intimate and personal side. It is shaped by the experiences in which we have lived. But it also has a social and public side. The old familiar mourning rituals which crystallized the experiences of past generations have disappeared from our 'culture of narcissism'.[2] Our society with its many suppressions doesn't want to permit experiences of death and mourning. But people who in their grieving are not prepared to let society push them on to the side-lines, will have to set out on their own path into the experience of mourning. They may find most help in the self-help groups for the bereaved. These don't offer any therapy, but they do offer mutual help and a new experience of the self in the solidarity of a community.

In the self-help groups of the bereaved, consolations in grief are discovered mutually, in conversation. This is very much in line with the old concept of the religious communities, which Luther took over, the *mutua consolatio fratrum,* the mutual consolation of the brethren. As brothers and sisters, men and women enter mutually into the situations of the others, and combine the trust which loosens dumb tongues with respect for the intimate mystery of the other person. Here no one talks down to anyone else. People speak or are silent, weep and laugh with others in the same situation. For those who set up the self-help groups, the important point is not to be theologically correct but to be personally concrete. It is not what is always right that can be 'applied'. The appropriate releasing and comforting word for the

particular situation has to be sought. To find it requires awareness and sensibility, and not least the experience one has oneself
worked through – especially the experience of one's own neglects
and the things in one's own life that have been left uncompleted.

Anyone who is profoundly affected by death, whether it be the
death of a child, a wife or husband or mother, is generally sub-
jected to pain of such violence that even those who are spiritually
strong lose their footing and are overwhelmed. In this situation it
is only out of the solidarity of suffering that they can be talked to
at all. And yet the people closest to them must keep their heads
above water and look beyond the moment of pain. Often the
pain comes over the grieving in waves. If this is so, the ability to
weep is better than a dumb, frozen calm. Even to lose consciousness can be a blessing in the pain of mourning.

If the pain comes in waves, the intervals between them must be
used to find the foothold from which lines of resistance can be
built up. One can try to elicit stories and pictures – memories in
which the pain can find expression and give the mourners com-
posure. This comfort is tied completely to the moment, and is
generally washed away again by the next wave of grief. A long
accompaniment is always necessary, and best of all a firm enfold-
ing community, before the reality of the beloved person's death
can be accepted without those affected being overwhelmed by
the pain, and without their repressing the pain, so that in their
inconsolability they can be consoled, and so that the lost person
can be kept present in the reawakened courage to live. As long as
we still miss the dead, they are beside us. 'Nothing can make up
for the absence of someone we love, and it would be wrong to try
to find a substitute; we must simply hold out and see it through.
That sounds very hard at first, but at the same time it is a great
comfort; for since the gap really remains unfilled, it keeps us
bound to one another.'[3]

In talking together, both sides, the accompanying and the
accompanied, experience something new. Those who accompany help the grieving, so as to support and encourage them, and
those accompanied teach the others by telling their own experiences. So the first question is not 'How can I help?', or 'What
shall I say?' but 'What does he or she want to tell me?' Listening
to each other and talking to each other then generates a dialogue

in the face of death and with the pain of grief, until the loss can be accepted and, through a transformation, a new community with the dead comes into being. Grief for the one lost can be transformed into gratitude for what has been experienced. The fellowship with the beloved person doesn't have to be broken off; it can be transformed in such as way that we live with them, just as formerly they were a part of our own lives, and the community shared with them does not have to be forgotten.

Mourning and Melancholia:
A Discussion with Sigmund Freud

'People who have lost someone intimately connected with them suffer a bereavement which for them can never be made good. They feel incomplete, left behind, and incapable of living alone. Through the death of a person close to them, which they often experience as an amputation, they have lost part of themselves. Not only half of life but half of their soul too has gone from them.'[4] In order to take this apt description further, and to find ways leading out of this loss of the self, we shall look at Freud's ideas about 'Mourning and Melancholia'.[5]

'Mourning is regularly the reaction to the loss of a loved person, or to the loss of some abstraction which has taken the place of one, such as fatherland, liberty, an ideal, and so on . . . It does not occur to us to regard mourning as a morbid condition. We feel sure that after a certain time it will be overcome. Consequently interference with mourning must be viewed as inexpedient and harmful.'

'The distinguishing mental features of melancholia are a profoundly painful dejection, abrogation of interest in the outside world, loss of the capacity to love, the inhibition of all activity, and a lowering of the self-regarding feelings which finds expression in self-reproaches and self-revilings, and culminates in a delusional expectation of punishment.'

According to this distinction between mourning and melancholia, there is mourning if a partnership existed and the person was loved for his or her own sake. Mourning consists of a slow detachment of the cathectic energies from the lost object of love.

After the completion of what German calls *Trauerarbeit*, 'the work of grief', the ego is once again free and able to choose a new object for its love.

In the case of someone suffering from melancholia, on the other hand, the experience of an exceptional lowering of the ego-feeling indicates that the choice of object was made on the basis of narcissistic self-love. The person loved was not loved for his or her own sake, but was the object of the projected needs, cravings for power, and wishful thinking of self-love. The narcissistic ego therefore reacts to the loss of the object of love with a sense of personal injury or affront. It feels that it has been left in the lurch and betrayed by the dead person. The libido's cathectic energies are withdrawn into the ego. Dissociations of the ego result and express themselves in self-hatred and melancholy. If they are repressed, the mental operations involved in the process of detachment from the beloved object take place mainly in the subconscious. This impedes the mastering of the conflict that has arisen in the self.

A first important point about Freud's distinction between mourning and melancholia is his distinction between a love which loves the object for its own sake, and the narcissistic love which in the object of love, loves and enjoys only him- or herself. This conforms to the ancient theological distinction between love of one's neighbour and self-love. The psychoanalytical figure of Narcissus, who fell in love with himself, corresponds to the figure which was used by Augustine and Luther, the figure of the *homo incurvatus in se* – the person turned in on himself. People who are in love with themselves are permanently afraid for themselves. They use all objects and experiences and every other person as mirrors of themselves, and for the purpose of self-endorsement. The object of love is viewed merely as a possession that 'belongs to me'. What they love in other people is only the resonance of their own selves. They only love those who are like themselves, not people who are 'other'. They love what corresponds to themselves and increases their experience of themselves, and what exalts their opinion of themselves: they don't love what is 'other', which seems to them merely strange and hostile. It is clear that loss of the object of love is then taken as personal injury.

In contrast, those who love other people for their own sake can mourn without melancholia. They accept the beloved person for his or her own sake, and make no possessive claims. In the language of faith: the people they love are accepted as a gift of God's love, so they can also be left to that eternal love when death comes. Through this gratitude, the joy of experiencing the happiness of love becomes a protection in the experience of grief. In the very consciousness of loss, gratitude keeps the fellowship with the beloved person alive.

Freud thinks that in 'the work of grief' the libido is withdrawn from the lost object of love, until the ego is capable of choosing something new to love. That sounds very mechanistic, and is not an adequate analysis of the complexity of human relationships. This pattern of thought leads to the conclusion that in love we should surrender ourselves only up to a certain point, so that we can withdraw our love again after disappointments, separations or in the case of death, in order then to choose a new object of love. This idea, again, presupposes a stable and at heart untouchable ego, which only gives itself up to relationships incidentally, or to a subsidiary degree. But isn't this an extremely narcissistic picture of the ego, which leads to a kind of permanent melancholia in the unloved and unlived life?

According to the accounts of the bereaved, however, and from my own experience, it would seem to me that when so-called 'objects of love' die, part of those who loved them dies too in spirit; in the death of the people they love, those who are left experience what death really is. Here it is not a matter of an injury to a narcissistic self-love, so this is not melancholia; it is part of the mourning process itself. 'The work of grief' does not merely serve to detach love from the 'object' it has lost, so that it is able to choose a new love. Of course that can also be the result. But at heart it is a matter of the renewal of the self which, by virtue of the love, has died with the beloved person. In the mourners themselves 'the well of life' opens again. They acquire a new will to live, and courage for new experiences of life. They won't forget the dead, but they can remember them without sinking into the bottomless pit of grief. Remembrance of the dead changes. The feeling of loss and the gap left in one's own life of course remains, but it is joined by the feeling of gratitude for the life shared and the happiness experienced. A certainty even comes into being that what has been still endures and cannot be destroyed. The past is past, and at the same time it is in its own way present, so that it ceases to be transitory. In grief we realize not only the present loss, but also that the dead have become an integral component of our own life history. Of course in our grief we take leave of them. But in faith we know that death is not final, and so we also discover that the parting does not have to be absolute. If we part from someone in the face of God, then it is parting in the enduring presence of eternity. We express this by saying that when we take leave of them, God has taken those we love to himself, for 'all live to him' (Luke 20.38). But then our leave-taking becomes different. It loses its tragic quality and its finality. In our grief we don't only take leave of the dead; we also participate in their transformation into that other world of God's, and that other life which we call eternal.

If death isn't the end, then mourning doesn't have to be endless either. If death is the side of the transformation to eternal life that is turned towards us, then our grief is transformed from mere lament over the loss into a new fellowship with the dead. If we believe that the dead experience resurrection, then this hope leads us out of the abyss of fear and makes us free. We look beyond the graves and the partings in our life to that new future of God's in which 'death shall be no more' (Rev. 21.4).

To keep company with the dead in backward-looking gratitude and forward-looking hope doesn't mean holding on to memories and clinging to the dead in such a way that we no longer have a life of our own. It is rather that the dead are present in a kind of second presence. In this singular presence, they don't bind life to themselves. They let it go free where it knew itself to be bound to them. On the other hand those who go on living musn't forget the dead, and mustn't withdraw their love from them so as to lead an independent life.

We have expanded Freud's analysis by drawing attention to the link between grief and gratitude on the one hand, and between mourning and hope on the other. This brings us back to the difference between mourning and melancholia, for in Freud's analysis of melancholia we find elements which can be found in every grief.

Human love for other people is always bound up with self-love, for not all self-love is narcissistic. The command to love our neighbour presupposes self-love: '. . . as yourself'. How can someone who hates himself love other people? Moreover love is a reciprocal affair. If I love her for her own sake, I know that I am loved by her for my own sake too. True love is more than an association for reciprocal use or mutual possession. The ego-impoverishment and the loss of self felt on the death of the beloved person are inescapable elements in the mourning process. They are by no means in themselves symptoms of melancholia. Of course all self-love, even the self-love experienced in being loved, also contains narcissistic elements of self-endorsement, vanity and fear. It would be inhuman to exclude them and to see them as being in themselves pathological.

The process of mourning and talk with other mourners will then make the grieving aware of what true love for others for their own sake is, and what being truly loved for one's own sake is, and what ministered only to self-endorsement, vanity and one's own fear. Grief leads the grieving to self-examination. It can make us aware of where we fell short towards the dead, and where the dead fell short towards us – aware too of what we had wanted to say to them, what we wanted to thank them for, or what we wanted to ask their forgiveness for. Every partnership always remains incomplete. But the self-examination can also make us conscious of the elements in our love which are true and enduring, and which elements were part of our narcissistic lovelessness and should therefore disappear.

Consolation and the Rebirth to Life

The pain of grief lies in the sense of loss and of being lost oneself. So consolation in grief is found in the experience of indestructible community, in the knowledge that the dead person is in safe-keeping with God. But this is only possible if the deity is not an unfeeling, indifferent heavenly power called 'fate', but is the eternal love that feels with us and suffers with us. We can then discover that our sorrow is God's sorrow too, and that hidden in the pain of our own love is a divine pain as well. God loves with those who love. God weeps with those who weep. God grieves with the grieving. So whoever remains in love even in the midst of grief and does not become bitter remains in God.

> And when human hearts are breaking
> under sorrow's iron rod,
> then we find that self-same aching
> deep within the heart of God.[6]

One of God's great promises according to the biblical writings is Jesus' beatitude: 'Blessed are those who mourn, for they shall be comforted' (Matt. 5.4; Isa. 61.2).

If mourners are Jesus' friends, as the Sermon on the Mount says, then he has become their divine friend. If they are comforted, then others find the consolation of God in their community with the sufferers. They share in their grief and wait with them for God's consolation. They 'bear' the suffering together.

In this way the community of Christ stands out against the culture of narcissism. It comes forward publicly for the recognition of mourners and respect for them, and it calls into life new public mourning rituals. It takes active part in the hospice movement.

Where and how will those who mourn be comforted?

I believe the answer is to be found in the great vision of Jewish and Christian hope with which we look beyond the grave and death into the future of God. 'God will wipe away every tear from their eyes, and death shall be no more, neither shall there be mourning nor crying nor pain any more, for the former things have passed away. And he who sits upon the throne says: Behold, I make all things new' (Rev. 21.4, 5; Isa. 35.10).

IX

The Community of the Living
and the Dead

The Ancestor Cult

Ideas about a life after death are important not only for the dying
but for the living too, who after the people they love have died
feel that they have been 'left behind'. Ideas about life after death
do not merely say something about our own fate; they always
also embrace our relations of fellowship with the dead, and
for the survivors who want to go on leading their lives in the
presence of those they have lost they are important.

In modern societies the individual consciousness of being oneself drives out the collective sense of existing within a succession
of generations. This destroys all community with the dead. The
dead are then 'dead' in the modern sense. That is, they no longer
exist, they no longer have any significance, and are no longer perceived. We no longer need to take account of our ancestors. They
no longer enrich our lives, and no longer trouble them. When
they died we told ourselves that 'life has to go on'. We didn't ask
what happened to the dead, but only what was to happen afterwards to the living. In this way, in modern societies the living
have come to dominate the dead.

In traditional societies, life is regulated by what the West and
the modern world often disparagingly term the 'ancestor cult'.[1]
This gives form to the community shared by ancestors and
descendants. The world of the ancestors is the other side of the
world of the living, and the greater side. Consequently the life of
those that come later must be slotted into the world of their
ancestors. Why and how that takes place we can see from the

account in a novel by Robert van Gulik, the Dutch diplomat and writer. He describes a Chinese judge living in the ninth-century T'ang era:

> Rising, the judge reverently opened the high double doors of the cupboard. The shelves were crowded with small, vertical wooden tablets, each standing on a miniature pedestal of carved wood. Those were the soul tablets of Judge Dee's ancestors, each marked in golden letters with their posthumous name and rank, and the year, day and hour of their birth and death.
>
> The judge knelt again, and touched the floor three times with his forehead. Then, with closed eyes, he concentrated his thoughts.
>
> The last time the ancestral shrine had been opened was twenty years ago, in Tai-yuan, when his father had announced to the ancestors Judge Dee's marriage with his First Lady. He had been kneeling with his bride behind his father. He saw before him the thin, white-bearded figure with the dear, wrinkled face . . .
>
> Across the vast expanse of the floor, at the back of the hall, he saw faintly the long robe, shimmering with gold, of the Grand Ancestor, sitting there motionless on his high throne. He had lived eight centuries ago, not long after the Sage Confucius . . .
>
> The judge spoke in a clear voice:
>
> 'The unworthy descendant of the illustrious house of Dee, named Jen-djieh, eldest son of the late Councillor Dee Cheng-yuan, respectfully reports that having failed in his duties to the state and the people, he will today tender his resignation'. . .
>
> As he fell silent, the vast assembly slowly faded away before his mind's eye.[2]

Ancestors are not dead in the modern sense of being no longer there. They continue to exist in the realm of spirits, and are so much present to the living that they know they are sustained by them and are answerable to them. All important family decisions are announced to them. At the New Year festival, the eldest son pays them reverence before the shrine. At the Chusok festival the community shared with them is celebrated at the graves of the dead. Ancestors can torment their descendents through their unrest, and bless them through their peace. Descendants live in awareness of the constant presence of those who have gone before them. Every decision that is of vital importance for living must be made before the succession of ancestors, because these decisions affect not only those living in the present and those that are to come, but also those that have gone before, especially with regard to the honour or shame which they can be caused. As the long register of generations in the Old Testament, and the century-long ancestor tablets in China and Korea show, the communities of the generations through time are an essential component of life itself. Here there is no individual identity without this collective continuity.

Hope for Those Who Have Gone Before

Is this veneration for ancestors a religious cult, or a self-evident part of reverence for life? That was the question facing the Christian missions to China at the end of the sixteenth century. The Jesuit missionary society, to which the famous Italian priest Matteo Ricci also belonged, found no contradiction between the Chinese ancestor cult, its Confucian basis and the Christian faith. But then Franciscans and Dominicans came and condemned this Chinese custom as idolatry. The Vatican decided this conflict in 1715 and 1741 through two edicts which condemned the Jesuit standpoint, and forbade any Christian acknowledgement of the ancestor cult.[3] But in 1939 Pope Pius XII proclaimed that at the present time the ancestor cult was not religious, and hence not idolatrous, but as a civil ceremony was quite compatible with the Christian faith.

This late change of heart was not entirely voluntary: the Japanese government had demanded that Christians within the Japanese sphere of interest should recognize Shinto, and hence also recognize Shinto as the national Japanese religion, in which the Tenno or emperor had to be worshipped as a god. So this Catholic recognition of the ancestor cult came about at the very time when ancestor veneration really did become political idolatry, so that Christian resistance was in fact called for. But there were enough martyrs at that time who because of their personal faith resisted the Japanese emperor cult. If the emperor of China is not a human being but 'the Son of Heaven', if the emperor of Japan is not a human being but a god, the result for Christians is the conflict which Jesus solved with the familiar saying: 'Render to Caesar the things that are Caesar's, and to God the things that are God's.' That is to say, God is God, and the emperor is a human being, which means that all that is due to him is respect conditioned by faith in God, and a limited obedience.

Can there be a Christian veneration for ancestors? Protestant missionaries in China, Korea and Japan have often termed the veneration for ancestors in general idolatry, and have demanded that every Christian should renounce his ancestors on baptism. But with this demand they have also fostered the individualism of Western culture, and have destroyed Asia's ancient family culture. It is better to develop specifically Christian forms of ancestor veneration, which make it possible for Christians in China, Korea and Japan to remain Chinese, Koreans and Japanese. Are there any theological reasons for a Christian veneration for ancestors – reasons which do not merely serve to bring Christians into line with Asiatic culture, but also lead to a reform of the Asiatic culture itself by way of Christians? There are two reasons.

1. 'For the unbelieving husband is consecrated through his wife, and the unbelieving wife is consecrated through her husband. Otherwise your children would be unclean, but as it is they are holy', writes Paul (1 Cor. 7.14), discussing the question whether Christians should separate from unbelieving partners. I believe that this vicarious sanctification can be extended to ancestors too. The faith of those who come later also acts as a sanctification for earlier generations of the families. Otherwise your ancestors would be unclean, but now they are holy: or so we might go on, in the spirit of the apostle. But if they are holy in this sense, then they can also be revered, and then the family's relationship to them is not severed just because their descendants have become Christians; it is sanctified. To sanctify the relationships with them means bringing them before the face of God and shaping these relationships under his blessing.

2. The community of Christ is a community not only of the living but of the dead as well. It is not just a community of 'brothers and sisters'; it is a community of mothers and daughters, and of fathers and sons – or of mothers and sons, and fathers and daughters. In Rom. 14.9 Paul writes: 'For to this end Christ died and lived again, that he might be Lord both of the dead and of the living.' His sovereignty over the dead is not yet the resurrection of the dead but is only as yet their saving reception into the community of Christ. When he 'descended into hell' (the realm of the dead), as the Creed puts it, Christ broke the power of death and took the dead into his fellowship. So the community of Christ is in him a community of the living with the dead, and of the dead with the living. In the risen Christ, the wall of death has been broken down. So in this community with Christ the dead are not 'dead' in the modern sense; they 'have a presence'. That is the element of truth in the Asiatic reverence for ancestors and for life in their presence. Christ's death and resurrection do not have a meaning only for the future of those living in the present; they also embrace hope for those in the past. The hope for the resurrection of the dead is the only hope we know which is related to those of the past. So in this hope the dead are already in safe keeping. Seen in the light of the resurrection, they are sanctified.

The prospect of resurrection is the new Christian light which falls on the reverence for ancestors, and which raises this to new level. In this light Christians in the modern Western world will also be able to turn hopefully to their dead, and through a new culture of remembrance surmount the compulsion to forget.

The closer we come to Christ the closer the dead come to us. In the worship of the Latin American base communities, the names of 'the disappeared' – the people murdered by the military dictatorships – are often called, and the congregation responds with the cry: 'Presente!' They are not 'disappeared', they are not dead; in Christ they are present and among us. In worship this is quite particularly the case in the eucharistic presence of Christ. That is the deeper reason for the Catholic Church's Masses for the dead. The dead are also present in what used to be called alms-giving. Here we find the presence of Christ among 'the least of my

brethren', according to Matthew 25: 'What you do to them you
do to me' and therefore also to the dead who are beside me.

Prayers for the Dead?

Ought we to pray for the dead? Because Israel's faith always
closed itself off particularly rigidly from the cults of the dead
practised in its environment, the Reformers, with their stress on
the Bible, saw no reason to continue with the medieval Church's
Masses for the dead and prayers for the dead. According to
Luther we should still pray a few times for the dead, but should
then leave them in Christ's keeping. According to Calvin, we
should no longer intervene in Christ's fellowship with the dead
through prayers. Modern revival preachers have often stressed to
the living the hour of decision for faith by using the threat that
without that decision one is lost after death, and that even
prayers no longer help. This emphasis led to a schism in the
Syrian Orthodox Church in Kerala, India, for example, since
prayers for the dead were retained by the Orthodox Church.

I myself do not believe that we can or must do something for
the salvation of the dead through our prayers. But I do believe
that the Christ risen from death also has his means of salvation
in the realm of death too. Otherwise death would be stronger
than Christ. In prayers for the dead we seek the community with
them which their death has severed for us on earth, but which is
preserved in the One who has taken away death's power. When
we pray for the dead, we also begin to live in their spiritual presence. In everything we do or suffer they look over our shoulders,
so to speak.

A good way of beginning to celebrate the community of the
living and the dead in Christ would then be to introduce a special
ritual of reconciliation at funerals. In order to find peace, we ask
God to forgive all our shortcomings towards those who have
died, and to forgive all their shortcomings towards us. Then we
can live with the dead in the peace of God. Then the living must
no longer be tormented by feelings of guilt and self-reproach,
and those belonging to the dead who will die later can find peace
in the relationships that made up their lives.

In countries with a developed tradition of veneration for ancestors, Christians are careful to see that reverence and gratitude are offered to them not merely by the eldest son but by daughters too, for all alike are baptized, and in Christ there is neither man nor woman, but all are one (Gal. 3.28).

The integration of the living in the world of those who have gone before them finds its equivalence in the integration of the dead in the world of their descendants, so that the outcome is a balanced continuity of the generations. The reason is that, from the Christian viewpoint, ancestors no longer appear in the light of a mythical origin, to which they are closer by virtue of their age than their descendants; now both those who have gone before and their descendants appear in the light of the future resurrection of the dead and the common hope for 'the life of the world to come'. Their community in Christ is a community of hope. In this hope a shared present comes into being, which reaches beyond the times that pass away.

The Culture of Remembrance

In the countries of the modern Western world we need a new culture of remembrance, in order no longer to live simply from day to day as individuals but to look beyond. The individualization of men and women has also led to a very short-term sense of time which takes in only the present. But if we relate time only to ourselves, we find ourselves short of time, for 'life is short', as we say. It is only if we again see our lifetime within the wider contexts of the generations and their history that we acquire time in remembering the past and in hoping for what is to come. The pressure of time is always related only to the present, and this pressure is then relaxed.

Because the sense of tradition which was once a matter of course has got lost, today we are searching for a 'generation contract'. By this we mean agreements between present and future generations which will even-out the utilization of natural resources and cultural chances for living. The really important decisions of the present must be made with an eye to coming generations; but these generations have no present lobby.

Among Native Americans decisions of this kind are supposed to be made with reference to seven coming generations. The modern world which sees only its own present is far removed from this wisdom.

The one side of the generation contract is closely dependent on the other. The person who forgets the rights of the dead will be indifferent towards the life of those who come later. So without a culture of remembrance modern culture will find no future either. But a culture without the vista of a future is an apocalyptic culture of downfall. The rediscovery of the community of the living with the dead can therefore also lead to an awareness of the community of the living with their children, and will free our glance for the future of modern society.

In the post-war years, we in Germany discovered particularly painfully and enduringly how necessary a culture of remembrance is, if we are to come to terms with the sins of the fathers which burden the life of their children. Anyone who saw on television the son of Hans Frank, the former *Gauleiter* of Poland, who was responsible for the mass murder of Jews and Poles, has sensed the burden this accursed name laid on the next generation. The son of the party leader Bormann became a Catholic priest and went to the Congo. The community of the living with the dead is not a way of providing the living with cheap comfort; it is a reality which has to be worked through in family therapy and psychoanalytically. It is here that prayer for the dead and in their stead has its *Sitz im Leben*, its place in life. The sins of the forefathers oppress the consciences of their descendants; the sufferings of parents weigh on the love of their children; the blessing of their ancestors fills the life of those to come. It is time to become conscious in the Western world of the community of the living and the dead.

X

What Awaits Us?

What we hope for and what we expect can be discerned from our wishes and intentions. But what awaits us during our lifetime we don't know. The future into which our wishes and intentions tentatively reach out is full of surprises, for good or ill. It makes sense to accept the fact, in confidence though circumspectly. But what awaits us after we die? Does anything await us at all? Must we die in complete ignorance, resigned to our fate? Or is a degree of curiosity justified? It may be good to fall back first of all on the 'basic trust' with which we entered life. That will carry us out of this life too. And if this basic trust has become for us trust in God, and if it was not prematurely destroyed, then of course we still don't know *what* awaits us, but we do know, surely, *who* awaits us. Why shouldn't we trust the one we have trusted throughout our life once our lifetime ends? Then we don't die into the eternal Nothingness or infinite silence; we die into the eternally bounteous God and the wide space of his creative love.

When we have arrived at this answer to the question: *Who* awaits me? the next question inescapably follows: *What* awaits us when we trust ourselves to God in this way? Will God encounter us as Judge or as Saviour, or as both together?

In this chapter we shall look critically at the traditional ideas about the Last Judgement, hell, the realm of the dead, and the restoration of all things, and shall try to formulate them afresh in line with faith in Christ.

What Awaits Us at the Last Judgement?

Throughout the ages, expectation of the great Judgement at the end of time has plunged human beings into fear and trembling. The earliest pictures of this judgement known to us do not belong to the Christian world but come from the Egypt of the Pharaohs. Here the great judge Osiris pronounces judgement, and Ma'at (Truth or Justice) weighs the souls according to their good and evil deeds.[1] In medieval Christian pictures Christ is seen sitting on the judgement throne with a double-edged sword in his mouth. The archangel Michael stands in front of him with the scales. Sometimes there is also a little devil who pulls down the scales on the side of evil, but a good angel keeps his hand on the other scale, so that no unjust judgement results. In this final judgement there are only two verdicts: eternal life or eternal death. On the right-hand side the angels carry off the righteous to heaven, on the left, devils drag the wicked down to hell. Since no one knows how righteous he or she has to be in order to get to heaven, the expectation of judgement evokes more fear and trembling in human beings than it awakens trust in God. Fear of hell then increases the fear of death in the dying, because it is no longer possible to put anything right: everyone must appear before the divine judgement seat with his or her life just as it has been. In some people this idea of judgement also intensifies their addiction to self-punishment. They put themselves in the judge's place and destroy themselves.

The image of the God who judges in wrath has caused a great deal of spiritual damage. The approach of the Last Judgement was always a threatening message used by the Church and some evangelists, and it poisoned the idea of God in the soul.[2] It plunged the one into profound self-doubt and roused the other to an outraged rejection of any belief in God at all.

Modern theological interpretations of Judgement have therefore put the personally responsible human being at the centre, instead of the wrathfully judging God: no one is sent to heaven or hell against his or her will. It is the person's own decision, which has one or the other consequence. Of course God comes to meet all human beings with love, but he also respects their response. Everyone has the chance finally to reject God and to enter the state of eternal God-forsakenness which used to be called hell. From this perspective – the perspective of the personally responsible human being – the Last Judgement appears to be simply the ultimate endorsement of our free will. 'No one is predestined by God to go to hell. Only a voluntary turning away from God, a deadly sin persisted in, leads to hell' says the new Universal Catechism of the Roman Catholic Church of 1992.[3]

Let us consider both ideas about the Last Judgement.

– If the judging God is at the centre, no one knows how righteous he or she has to be. Everyone is delivered over to the unknown judgement of God.

– If the responsible human being is at the centre, no one knows what future he or she will arrive at, because voluntary human decisions can vacillate.

– If the God of wrath is at the centre of judgement, we must despair of God; if the freely deciding human being is at the centre, each of us must despair of him- or herself.

– According to both ideas, human beings are really the masters of their own fate, or their own executioners. In both cases the role of God is reduced to that of executor or accomplice of the human being's free choice. Heaven and hell become religious images which endorse human free will.

– Whether the judging God or the responsible human being is at the centre, nothing Christian can be detected in these ideas. We find them in exactly the same way in the ancient Egyptian Book of the Dead, in the Koran, or in the Chinese myth of the Ten Judges of the Dead.

There is another approach to the idea of the great Last Judgement. Injustice cries out to high heaven. The victims who have suffered from it do not hold their peace. The perpetrators who have caused the suffering find no rest. The hunger for justice and righteousness remains a torment on both sides. The victims must not be forgotten, the murderers must not finally triumph over them. The expectation of a final universal judgement in which justice will finally triumph was originally a hope cherished by the victims of violence and injustice. It was their counter-history to the world of the triumphal evil-doers. They hoped for the final Judge 'who will establish justice for those who suffer wrong'. To this the psalms of lament in the Old Testament are an eloquent witness. It was only later and under other influences that this saving Judge of the victims became the judge of a criminal court before whom the evil-doers had to appear. The expectation of saving justice orientated towards the victims turned into a moral judgement orientated towards the perpetrators on the motto of 'measure for measure': the retributive justice in which good is repaid by good, and evil by evil. In order to Christianize the ideas about the Last Judgement, we are assuming that the ideas of judgement in the Bible developed out of the particular historical experience of the God of Israel's justice within the framework of the covenant, and not from the general principle of retributive justice.

Who is the Judge? According to the Christian ideas of the New Testament, Judgement Day is 'the Day of the Son of man' who came 'to seek that which was lost'. It is in fact 'the day of Jesus Christ' (Phil. 1.6). It is to be the day when the crucified Christ will be manifested to the whole world, and the whole world will be manifested before him. 'We must all appear before the judgement seat of Christ' (2 Cor. 5.10). On that day both will emerge from their concealment into the light of truth, the Christ who is now hidden, and the human being who is hidden from himself. The eternal light will reveal Christ and human beings to each other. What is now still hidden in nature will also become clear and lucid, for as bodily and natural beings men and women cannot be isolated from nature, not even before the face of God and at the Judgement.

According to what righteousness will Christ judge when he comes and is manifested as the Son of man-judge of the world? Surely this righteousness will be no different from the righteousness he himself proclaimed in his gospel and practised in fellowship with sinners and the sick! Otherwise no one would be able to recognize him. The coming Judge is the one who was put to death on the cross. The one who will come as Judge of the world is the one 'who bears the sins of the world' and who has himself suffered the suffering of the victims. When we look at the Judge in many medieval pictures, we would hardly just by ourselves arrive at the idea that he could be Jesus of Nazareth, the crucified one, and least of all if we look at that hero belonging to the ancient world in Michelangelo's famous picture in the Sistine Chapel.

The justice which Christ will bring about for all and everything is not the justice that establishes what is good and evil, and the retributive justice which rewards the good and punishes the wicked. It is *God's creative justice,* which brings the victims justice and puts the perpetrators right. The victims of injustice and violence are first judged so that they may receive justice. The perpetrators of evil will afterwards experience the justice that puts things to rights. They will thereby be transformed inasmuch as they will be redeemed only together with their victims. They will be saved through the crucified Christ, who comes to them together with their victims. They will 'die' to their evil acts and the burden of their guilt in order to be born again to a new life together with their victims. Paul also expresses this with the image of the fire through which every human work is proved: 'If any man's work is burned up, he will suffer loss, though he himself will be saved, but only as through fire' (1 Cor. 3.15). The image of the End-time 'fire' is an image of the consuming love of God. Everything which is, and has been, in contradiction to God will be burnt away, so that the person who is loved by God is saved, and everything which is, and has been, in accord with God in that person's life is preserved.

As the coming judge of victims and perpetrators, the risen Christ will do away with the suffering of the one and the burden of the other, and will bring both out of the dominion of evil into the community of God's righteousness and justice. The purpose of his judgement is not reward or punishment, but the victory of the divine creative righteousness and justice, and this victory does not lead to heaven or hell but to God's great day of reconciliation on this earth. On that day 'every tear will be wiped from their eyes', the tears of suffering as well as the tears of remorse, for 'there will be no more mourning, nor crying nor pain any more' (Rev. 21.4). Judgement is not the last thing of all. It serves the new creation of all things. It is therefore not last but penultimate. What is last and final is the new word of creation: 'Behold, I make all things new' (Rev. 21.5).

Of course the evil committed and suffered is not always distributed between different people and separate groups of people.

Victims can also become perpetrators, and in many people the perpetrator side of evil and the victim side are indistinguishably interlocked. It is all the more important to perceive that the coming Judge casts us down as perpetrators and raises us up as victims, and in this way also reconciles us with ourselves. But his judgement is always a *social* judgement.[4] The accused do not stand solitary and alone before their judge, as they do in human criminal courts, and in solitary torments of conscience. The victims stand there together with the perpetrators, and the perpetrators with the victims, Cain with Abel, Israel with the nations, the rich with the poor, the violent with the helpless, the martyrs with their murderers. The history of human suffering is indissolubly bound up with its history of guilt. The conflicts in which the one becomes the victim and the other the perpetrator are always social and political conflicts which are unsolved or unsolvable.

In Israel's histories with God, God's justice is invoked with the words: 'May the Lord judge between you and me!' (Gen. 16.5; 31.53; 1 Sam. 24,13). In these conflicts God is invoked as *justice of the peace*. That is the way he is to judge between the poor and the rich, the high and the low: 'Behold, I judge between sheep and sheep, rams and he-goats' (Ezek. 34.17), so that the herd can again live in peace. The petitioners in the psalms are also calling for judgement in social life with their tormenting question why everything goes right for the godless while those who are faithful to God are persecuted. God should judge between believers and the godless. A social judgement is to put right the relationships between human beings which have been disrupted through evil; the purpose is not to reward or punish individuals. God will 'put things to rights'.

According to the Israelite and Christian experiences of God, we ought to think of the Last Judgement too as proceedings held before a 'justice of the peace', not a criminal court. If the point of the final Judgement is to put right the relationships of community which have been disrupted, then in the coming Judge we expect a 'justice of the peace'. Where ideas of punishment are used in the New Testament, we shall interpret them in the light of the new creation of all things, which the Judgement is designed to serve. 'Judgement does not have a merely negative sense but above all a positive one. That is, it will not only destroy but will above all save; it will not merely dissolve but will above all fulfil. It is the annihilating No to all the powers hostile to God, and is the dissolution of the world of evil; but it is the saving and fulfilling Yes of creation: "Behold, I make all things new!" '.[5]

If judgement in the final Judgement is a social judgement, then it is a *cosmic* judgement too. All the disrupted conditions in creation must be put right so that the new creation can stand and endure on the ground of justice. That means the relations between human beings we have talked about, but it also means the relationship between the human race and the world of the living, and between the human race and the earth. The Messiah's kingdom of peace as it is seen in Isaiah 11 will bring justice for 'the poor'and such a peace in the world of nature that 'the wolf will lie down by the lamb and the lion will eat straw like the ox'. Darwin's struggle for existence will then give way to peace in existence.

Not least, 'the first creation' is a creation threatened everywhere by chaos. According to the picture language of the Bible, chaos thrusts into the creation of light and the earth in the form of 'night' and 'the sea'. This 'first thing' is to pass away (Rev. 21.1, 5). According to John's vision, the new creation of all things will no longer know any 'night' or 'sea', because God's radiant glory will illumine everything, and all created being will participate in God's being and his eternal life. That is a fundamental change in the constitution of earthly life and of the cosmos itself.

What will be annihilated is Nothingness, what will be slain is death, what will be dissolved is the power of evil, what will be separated from all created beings is separation from God, sin. The ground is then prepared for the new creation of all things.

Does Hell Threaten?

The fascination of wickedness has again and again evoked appalling visions of hell. The abominations of hell's torments were painted by medieval painters with obvious pleasure. Even today, little makes such a public sensation as discussions in the churches about hell. 'Is there fire in hell?' In 1962 this question was hotly discussed in the Norwegian press, until even the German magazine *Stern* took up this profound theological question. When in 1995 the Doctrine Commission of the Church of England in a general document did away with hell, replacing it by 'total non-being', the whole English press entered into the question, although this proposition was mentioned only in passing, in a paragraph about final judgement. In the same year, the church press in Germany took over this nonsensical question, fundamentalist theologians insisting that hell must not be shaken. Official quarters in the Protestant churches in Germany made it known that Article 17 of the Augsburg Confession still held good: 'That our Lord Jesus Christ will return on the last day for judgment and will raise up all the dead, to give eternal life and everlasting joy to believers and the elect, but to condemn ungodly men and the devil to hell and eternal punishment.'[6]

What are we to think about hell, in the light of this Church tradition? It is nothing other than the *religious torture chamber*. There the devil and the damned have to suffer 'eternal torment'. According to the Byzantine Father Chrysostom, hell is 'the land of eternal death in which there is no life, the place of darkness in which there is no light, an abyss out of which the sighs of the damned rise up without their finding anyone to hear them.' 'There all the senses are tormented', explains Gottfried Büchner's old *Hand-Konkordanz zum Neuen Testament* (1750; 29th ed. 1927), 'sight through eternal darkness, hearing through weeping and the gnashing of teeth, smell through the stink of sulphur, taste through the bitterness of eternal death, feeling through eternal torment.' This hellish torture has no end. This hell fire is unquenchable. There is no escape. The earthly torture chambers of the oppressors have apparently been based on the religious model of hell. But from these earthly tortures the tortured can escape through death, whereas cruel apocalyptic fantasy knows of no way out and no limits: the torments of hell are to last for ever, the fire of hell is to be unquenchable. The absurd thing is that although the tormented are supposed to be in 'the land of eternal death', they are apparently immortal. Although they are dead, they are supposed still to have the use of all their senses, so that they can be physically tormented.

Today the torments of hell are hardly painted in the churches in this terrifying way. If the aim is to stress the responsibility of men and women, the phrase used is 'inescapable distance from God', If this damnation is seen as God's own act, 'God-forsakenness' is thought to be the more appropriate expression. Hell then means the state of being excluded from fellowship with God, an exclusion either self-imposed or imposed by God himself.

General concepts of this kind and similar vividly embroidered images of the negative can be found in all religions. They are not Christian, even if Christian churches have taken them over. The only Christian thing is to look at the fate of Christ, and to ask on the basis of his experiences about what is called hell. Luther offers convincing advice: 'Thou must look upon hell and the eternity of torment not in thyself, not in themselves, not in those who are damned . . . Look upon the heavenly picture of Christ who for thy sake descended into hell and was forsaken by God as one eternally damned, as he said on the cross: O my God, why hast thou forsaken me? See, in that picture thy hell is conquered and thy uncertain election made sure. Seek thyself only in Christ and not in thyself, so wilt thou eternally find thyself in him.'[7] For Luther, hell is not some place in the beyond, in the underworld or in the abyss of evil. It is an experience of God. It is the experience of God-forsakenness. What Jesus suffered from Gethsemane to Golgotha – that was his descent into hell. Calvin interpreted Christ's descent into hell in the same way: in his suffering and dying, Christ experienced God-forsakenness, eternal damnation and eternal death. What we can with certainty call hell can be seen solely in Christ's passion. In his suffering from God, all assailed and God-forsaken men and women can find themselves again when they suffer the torments of hell here, before they die.

This descent of Christ's into hell *before* and *in* his death is followed by his descent into hell *after* his death and *before* his resurrection, according to the creed. Why should Christ have descended into hell and have entered the realm of the dead? His resurrection from the dead supplies the answer: he descended into hell, first, in order to open hell and to destroy the gates of hell; and he did so, second, in order to proclaim to the dead the gospel of their salvation.

According to this Christian view, neither God nor human beings decide about hell, but Christ alone: 'I died, and behold I am alive for evermore, and I have the keys of death and hell' (Rev. 1.18). What is Christ going to do with 'the keys of hell'? 'Christ hath burst the gates of hell', says Charles Wesley in his Easter hymn.[8] So all its gates are open. Hell is no longer inescapable, and in hell no one must 'abandon hope', as Dante told the damned they must do. In trust in Christ's redeeming 'descent into hell', each of us can expect with Psalm 139.8 that 'though I make my bed in hell, thou art there', and can sing with the first Easter hymn which Paul quotes in 1 Cor. 15.55: 'O Hell where is thy victory?' If there were still any lost in hell, it would be a tragedy for Christ, who came 'to seek that which is lost'.[9]

If by virtue of Christ's resurrection this is true of hell *after* death, then it is all the more true for experiences of hell *before* death and for everything that 'makes life hell' for us, as we say. Even in the torture chambers of this world, the assailed and tortured Christ is present and delivers us from our fears: 'Nought from us his love shall sever; / life nor death, nor powers of hell / tear us from his keeping ever' writes the eighteenth-century poet Gellert.[10] And just this is the experience of men and women in their resistance against tyranny.[11] So we shall not be afraid of hell, nor, certainly, shall we threaten anyone else with hell.

Is There Salvation for the Dead?

The modern, ecumenical German version of the Apostles' Creed has replaced 'he descended into hell' by 'he descended into the realm of death'. For many people this sounds obscure and incomprehensible. Why should Christ enter the world of the dead? Does his death have a meaning for those who have already died? The First Epistle of Peter (3.18–22; 4.6) talks about Christ's proclamation of the gospel to the dead in the life-giving Spirit of the resurrection. By this the writer means first of all the dead 'who formerly did not obey, when God's patience waited', but then all the dead too, so that 'they might live in the spirit of God'. We are not told how that can come about, whether the dead hear the gospel of Christ and, like the living, can arrive at faith. For us, it is enough, after all, to know that death can set no limits to the saving gospel of Christ, and that in faith in Christ there is hope for the dead too. For us who are still alive they are of course dead, so that we cannot do anything more for them, but for the risen Christ they are not dead in this sense. He is beside them. He can do something for them. He has his own possibilities for them. And he does something for them. He will not finally give them over to eternal death. He descends into 'the realm of death', in order to make it his own kingdom and to fill it with his life. It is therefore important to perceive that this descent into the realm of the dead is the first act in his resurrection. As the one 'put to death in the flesh, but made alive in the Spirit' (3.18) Christ comes to the dead.

The wonderful Orthodox resurrection icon shows the risen Christ as the head of the new humanity. He is holding Adam and Eve by the hand, and pulling them with him out of the world of the dead. The Orthodox liturgy runs: 'Everything is now filled with light, heaven and earth and the realm of death. The whole creation rejoices in Christ's resurrection.' So Christ 'descended into the realm of death' in order to fill it with the jubilation of the resurrection. The night of death gives way to the daybreak colours of the resurrection. Anyone who thinks of the dead with Christ, doesn't look to their past, which cannot be brought back, but to their hoped-for future. The pain of separation finds consolation in the hope for reunion.

'The Restoration of All Things'

In a letter written from prison to his friend Eberhard Bethge, Bonhoeffer wrote at Christmas 1943: 'Nothing that is past is lost . . . God gathers up again with us our past, which belongs to us . . . Everything is taken up in Christ . . . Christ restores all this as God originally intended it to be.'[12]

If Christ is to bring everything again, then nothing can be lost to him, not even that which we cannot hold on to here. What we have loved, what we miss, will return again in his future, for the resurrection is stronger than death. Everything which is divided by death will be found again in the resurrection. I find this hope very comforting, for it makes us ready to let go what we cannot hold on to, and gives us the strength to live with the pain of separation and forsakenness. The separation from the people we love and the forsakenness which love experiences are not the end, for they are not the last of all.

But the idea of a 'restoration of all things' goes beyond this personal consolation. It has cosmic dimensions. In eighteenth-century German Pietism, this idea comes to the fore in expectation for the cosmos.[13] In Württemberg, Johann Albrecht Bengel and Friedrich Christoph Oetinger, Michael Hahn and both the Blumhardts developed it, backing it up with biblical evidence. If, as in Paul's vision, God will in the end be 'all in all' (1 Cor. 15.28), then nothing present and nothing past is excluded. We are told that in the fulfilment of the times all things will be united in Christ, things in heaven and things in earth' (Eph. 1.10) and 'all things reconciled to him, whether on earth or in heaven' (Col. 1.20), because 'all things were created through him' (Col. 1.16); and if this is so, we have to talk about the universality of God's grace. 'Every tongue shall confess that Jesus Christ is Lord, to the glory of God the Father' (Phil. 2.11). Then 'universal reconciliation' can no longer be a heresy and a reproach. It is an expression of hope and of trust in God's goodness. But the decision is God's alone.

The main point of the doctrine about the restoration of all things is not the reconciliation and redemption of all human beings, however. The doctrine is primarily concerned with 'all things', that is to say with everything created in heaven and on earth. All human doing and suffering is kept and remains in the eternal memory of God, and in the same way the history of creation is etched into his memory and preserved for its consummation in the eternal kingdom of his glory. In the restoration of all things, everything that happened in sequence in the progress of time will be present in the eternal moment. It is only then that what God promises in Rev. 21.5 can come to fulfilment: 'Behold I make *all things* new.'

The traditional doctrine about the Last Judgement also talks about a restoration, but it refers only to all human beings, the purpose being that all of them, beginning with Adam and Eve, can receive their just verdict. Afterwards only heaven and earth are left. The earth will be superfluous and is to be burnt. This notion of judgement is exceedingly hostile to creation. More: it is hostile to human beings too, for human beings are earthly creatures (Gen. 2.7) and without the earth cannot live. What business do we have in heaven among the angels? Human beings are not candidates for angelic status. They are the image of God on earth. Consequently we cannot talk about the new creation of human beings without talking about the new creation of the earth. There is no eternal life without 'the life of the world to come' and this world to come consists of new living spaces for dwellers in heaven and earth in 'the new heaven and the new earth in which righteousness dwells' (2 Peter 3.13). There cannot be salvation for human beings without 'the new earth'.

The idea about the restoration of all things shows very well the comprehensive dimensions of hope for the coming of the creative God; it is a hope which embraces the whole world. But the idea does not yet in itself say anything about the purpose of this restoration. That purpose cannot be the restoration of their original state, in the sense, perhaps, of the return of paradise. In that case the next Fall would already be pre-programmed. The raising of Christ from the dead was not, either, a 'return' of the life he had lived; it was a transformation of his life on earth into eternal life. And it is in this light that we ought to imagine the design of the restoration of all things: its purpose is the transformation of this world into the future world of the eternal creation. The restoration of all things is to initiate the rebirth of the cosmos to its enduring form.

XI

Eternal Life

What Are We Asking About?

Our personal lives are finite, mortal and brief. Final and mortal is the human race as well. It came late on the scene, and can disappear again early on, whether through natural catastrophes or through self-annihilation. Everything living which, in the course of evolution, has come into being on this fruitful planet earth, is ultimately speaking transitory. The earth itself may perish in a death of heat or cold, but at all events it will not remain as it is. How can there ever be an eternal 'life of the world to come'?

Before we look for an answer, we must clarify the question, and eliminate what we are not asking about. An 'eternal life' can hardly mean an endless prolongation of this one. Today's medical and biogenetic work on the prolongation of life has nothing whatsoever to do with what in religion is called 'eternal life', for eternity is not endlessness. An endless life of the kind we have here on earth would be without content, and one huge yawn. It would hardly be desirable, after all, to have to listen one day to professors who were 400 years old! Fredrick the Great was of course merely being cynical when he cried to the soldiers on his battlefield: 'Rascals, will you live for ever?', hoping thereby to hound them to a hero's death. But on the other hand eternal life cannot consist of the eternalization of the brief life lived here, for then nothing new could be expected of eternity, but merely the ultimate end of this life and – in the phrase so often used – 'eternal rest'. But isn't that rather 'eternal death'?

We are taking a step further if we talk not just about eternal life but also about an *eternal livingness*, so as to stop thinking of an extension of this life in the sense of longevity, and to think instead of the intensity of experience.[1] In this sense Friedrich Nietzsche was right when he wrote:

For all delight desires eternity,
Deep, deep eternity.[2]

It is not length of life in terms of time which reaches out to the originality which when we think God we call eternity; it is the depth of experience in the moment. Chronological time has nothing to do with this eternity of God's. But the fulfilled moment is like an atom of eternity, and its illumination is like a spark of the eternal light.

It is love which makes life truly living and disseminates delight in living. Out of delight in a life we love, we ask about the fullness of life, and call that 'eternal life'.

But when someone talks about eternal life today, everyone immediately thinks of a life after death. That life there is supposed to be a counter-image to life here: here life is transient, there everlasting; here mortal, there immortal; here temporal, there eternal. Nor is this confrontation between the positive there and the negative here wrong. We need counter-images of this kind, so that we do not come to terms with the disappointments and impairments of this life, but remain truly alive in our protest against them. If we trust in eternal life there, this impoverished and mortal life here can become more bearable – but it can become more unbearable too: implicit in the consolation of eternal life is always a protest also against the death of this life. But all too often, the hope for a fulfilled life 'there' draws off love from this life here, so that people feel that life here is like a waiting room for eternity, and only participate in it half-heartedly. So it is useful to be clear about both sides of this present life:

Life here and now is a life in time, that is true. But temporal life is not just a *transitory* life. It appears to us only as transitory to the extent to which we look to the past, and are forced to say farewell to what we cannot hold on to. But it is at the same time a life that *begins* every moment, and an awakening vitality, provided that we look to the future and welcome the possibilities of the new morning. Every moment in life is an end of the past and a beginning of the future. If we only have our death before our eyes, the impression that all the things we love are transitory

gains the upper hand. If we look beyond, and through, the dark
horizon of dying into the daybreak colours of God's new day,
then the 'beginningness' of all the things we love makes us living,
and it is to this beginningness that we are attentive.

Transitory life is life that is condemned to death. Life as beginning is life blessed with future. The original livingness has before
it the fulfilled life as its future hope. Fulfilled life is the name we
give to a life that is at one with itself, and is so interpenetrated by
the Yes to life that the poisonous bacilli of the negative are
excluded. It has to be a life in eternal present, without being-that-
is-no-more and without being-that-is-not-yet, without life that
has been passed over unlived, and without life that is merely
dreamed of. Then we no longer cling to our memories or live in
the illusory worlds of our desires, but are completely and wholly
there.

The livingness of the beginning points beyond itself by virtue
of its longing for happiness in life, and is itself a lived promise of
the life that is eternal. It is a visible parable of its own future
fulfilment. Can eternal life already be experienced here? Yes
indeed: passionate love and the joy in living taste of a livingness
that is primal, and strong as death. We can discern this power of
life with all our senses: 'Its embers are fiery and a flame of the
Lord' (Song of Solomon 8.6).

'God created man for eternal life', say Israel's wisdom (Wis.
2.23). If this is true, then human beings cannot come to terms
with this frail and dying life. They are destined for more. Their
will to live goes beyond the frontiers of this life. 'I am, but I do
not possess myself.'[3] 'I want to live but life slips away from me.'[4]
In me life did not succeed in arriving at a full and rounded-off
expression. This generates an inward unrest, which thrusts
beyond every condition of life that has already been reached.
This interest in life has also been called the human striving for
happiness. Yet nothing transitory can satisfy this striving, and
the restless human heart. The human 'soul' – that which 'ensouls'
human beings their life long – is this inner seeking and forward-
thrusting, this sense of inner emptiness and this search for the
fullness of life. The human being is an erotic being, moved by
sufferings and passions. The human being is a being full of
curiosity, enticed by wide horizons to set forth.

Of course this picture of the human being is a European one, shaped by the biblical books of God's promises and human departures into an unknown future. For a German, this is the 'eternal Faust' in us, but for an Indio it is the threatening Vasco da Gama mentality of the Spanish conquerors. Yet behind the cultural differences between the being-in-conflict here and the being-in-harmony there, we see in all human beings a surplus of driving force which presses forward towards fulfilment.[5]

How Can Human Life Become Eternal?

Since human beings are created beings and not gods, they will find the complete fullness of life not in themselves but only in the God who created them. Only in God is that eternally primal livingness to be found, and only in God the beauty which promises not merely happiness but also eternal bliss. Only in God is there both movement and rest, creative inexhaustibility and at the same time reposing perfection and completion. That is why Christian tradition has seen in God himself the 'highest good' (*summum bonum*) which at the beginning awakens all human striving and impelling, and in the end fulfils it. This finds expression in the hope for the contemplation of God which gives bliss (the *visio beatifica*) and in the expectation that when the goal is reached the God who has created everything and redeemed everything will so *indwell* his creation and be so enduringly present in it that he will be 'all in all' (1 Cor. 15. 28). We shall look at both visions of hope.

The *contemplation of God* is thought of as the beholding of God 'face to face' (1 Cor. 13.12). To make this possible the veil of hiddenness which now divides God and human beings must be put aside.[6] On God's side, this is his final manifestation of himself in his glory. On the side of human beings, it is purity of heart (Matt. 5.8) and the unveiled face which alone make it possible to behold God and live. What hides God and human beings from each other is not only that which makes the hidden God for us mysterious, and often enough so tormenting; it is also a grace: as we are now, we would perish before the radiant light of his glory. The story of Moses relates this very vividly (Ex. 33). The Lord comes down in the 'pillar of cloud' from his heights into the people of Israel's little 'tent of meeting' and 'speaks with Moses face to face as a man speaks to his friend'. The Lord then gives Moses 'a place beside him', and puts him into a cleft of rock, covering him with his hand, so that Moses can look upon God's glory after it has passed by, for 'my face shall not be seen' (33.23). The Hebrew Bible calls people to whom something of this kind happens 'friends of God'. In the New Testament, believers who have seen 'the glory of God in the face of Christ' (2 Cor. 4.6) are called 'friends' (John 15.15). In the light of God's Spirit, 'we all, with unveiled face, beholding the glory of the Lord, will be changed into his likeness from one degree of glory to another' (2 Cor. 3.18). How does this happen, and what happens to the human being in the process?

In contemplation we forget ourselves and in wonder are absorbed entirely into what we see. We do not appropriate our counterpart for ourselves, but give ourselves to our counterpart. In this way we ourselves are transformed through the contemplation, and through correspondences become similar to the one we see. Through contemplation we participate in, and become part of, the one contemplated. The contemplation of God confers an eternal *fellowship with God*.

The picture of wondering and beholding images the highest form of *love* of God: the love of God for his own sake. Whereas our gratitude is related to God's good gifts, contemplation apperceives God for his own sake. The contemplation of God makes the one who contemplates wholly self-forgetful, but not self-less. Those who look upon God do not lose themselves like drops in the infinite sea of the Deity, as Christian mystics have thought. Nor are they dissolved in a Nirvana, as Buddhists desire. They are still themselves and remain persons; otherwise there would no longer be any counterpart to the God who is looked upon, and the contemplation of God would have no contemplating subject. Love unites and distinguishes. It unites those who are different, and respects their unique character.

In biblical language, this being a counterpart to God is stressed by saying that there is to be a *mutual knowing*, face to face: we know God as we are known by him. Before we 'look upon' God, God looks at us: 'He sees everything under the heavens' (Job

28.24). So in contemplating God, human beings do not become gods themselves. But they are 'deified' inasmuch as they participate directly and without tormenting differences in God's primality and livingness, his truth and beauty. In their contemplation of God they receive as finite beings a *relative eternity*, by virtue of their unhindered participation in the divine eternity. It is a *participatory eternity*, into which human life is absorbed, and yet in God remains human.

According to Augustine, the contemplation of God leads to the full *enjoyment of God (fruitio Dei)*. It is not only the eyes which in bliss perceive what was hidden. All the senses are to perceive God's Deity, so that the completion is entire enjoyment in the fulfilment of every true human desire. It is only then that it is possible to speak about an *eternal bliss* and not only about an eternal life. Eternal bliss has the wondrous enjoyment of God as its content, and that exceeds every earthly happiness through its never-ending jubilation.

This enjoyment of God must also be imagined as a *mutual rejoicing*: human beings delight in their joy in God, and God 'is glad in his people' (Isa. 65.19). Created beings enjoy their fellowship with their Creator and the Creator enjoys his fellowship with the created beings who wholly correspond to him. The enjoyment of God is not thought of as something for individual souls. That is why Augustine talked about the mutual enjoyment of the human beings who enjoy God: *fruitio et seinvicem in Deo*. In their joy in God, human beings become a joy and enjoyment for each other – which we cannot say is always the case here and now. The direct fellowship with God leads to a direct fellowship of human beings with each other. Consequently the contemplation of God should not be understood merely in personal terms but socially too: people perceive one another and know one another 'in God'. That is much more than the 'seeing again' which many of the bereaved ask about.

In the idea about the all-perfecting and blissful *contemplation of God,* everything is so much directed to God himself that we get the impression that God in his infinite breadth is himself *the eternal home of everything* he has created. In the consummation, everything in its unique character (and therefore without losing itself) will dwell within the Deity beyond – not just the soul but the whole person, not just individuals but the whole community, not just human beings but all created beings in heaven and on earth. In the end God gathers everything into himself.

But this picture is one-sided. Just as in contemplation *every-thing* is *in God*, so *God*, for his part, *is present in all things*, and interpenetrates their finitude with his infinity. For this Paul takes the image: 'God will be all in all' (1 Cor. 15.28). That is the vision of God's kingdom in his glory. The divine and the earthly are not intermingled, the divine is not pantheistically absorbed into all things, but the divine and the earthly interpenetrate each other mutually: unmingled and undivided. That is the vision of *God's indwelling* in this world. The Creator does not remain detached from his creation. He enters into it, so as to make it his eternal dwelling. The whole creation becomes the temple of the Eternal One. Through this indwelling God interpenetrates every-thing with his livingness and his beauty, and all things will there-by be newly formed so that they conform to God and correspond to him in eternity. This new world will then become *God's eternal home country*, 'on earth as it is in heaven'.

What will then be different in the world? If God is in all things, then creativeness is present in everything created, and the infinite is present in everything finite. Then in everything we taste and see 'that the Lord is good'. Everything has the fragrance and taste of God because everything has then become the *sacrament of God*. That is what is meant by the eternal 'life of the world to come'. This sacramental view of the world is the necessary complement to the joyful contemplation of God.

If we call this new world in which nature and history are per-fected 'the kingdom of God', we must not interpret this kingdom theocratically, as the phrase would seem to suggest, but must stress the reciprocal interpenetration of God and world: God dwells in the world in a divine way, and the world dwells in God in a worldly way. The model for this view of the kingdom of God is Christ himself, for Christ is 'the kingdom of God in person', as the New Testament emphasizes: 'In him the whole fullness of deity dwells bodily' (Col. 2.9). What we have to expect of the coming kingdom of God on earth as it is in heaven is nothing less than the cosmic incarnation of God, in which divinity and humanity interpenetrate one another mutually as they do in the 'incarnation' of the eternal Word of God and in the 'outpouring of God's Spirit on all flesh'. According to Hebrew usage, the expression 'all flesh' means all the living. Earlier, the German version of the Apostles' Creed used the phrase 'the resurrection of the flesh'. And that means the eternal livingness of all the living.

The Time of Eternal Life

How are we to imagine a 'new livingness' if there is no more time? Or can the time of this life be so transformed that we can talk about an *eternal time* which corresponds to 'eternal livingness'? In the theological traditions there is in fact not only an awareness of the contrast between time and eternity; a differentiation is also made between 'the time of this world' and 'the time of the world to come'. The time of this world is the time of transience, the time of the future world is the time of the world that endures and is hence eternal. Further, a distinction is made between eternity as an attribute of God, the eternity that obtains in heaven and is an attribute of the angels, and the temporality of the earth and its inhabitants. Earthly time is the *chronological time* of becoming and passing away; heavenly time is the *aeonic time* of a relative eternity; the eternity of God is unique. If we look at aeonic time more closely, we find in its structure the cycles of time which were always viewed as a reflection of eternity: the circle without beginning or end is the figure of a *reversible time*, which distinguishes no past and no future, and yet does not stand still but moves in a circular course. Recurring movements of this kind stabilize life on earth and in the human organism, and provide duration and continuance in the stream of transience. In the outside world, we may think of the revolution of the earth, the earth's orbit round the sun, day and night, summer and winter; while within the human organism we have the circulation of the blood and the other circulatory movements.

If, therefore, eternal life is undisturbed participation in God's eternity, its own eternity is aeonic time. If this participation in the eternity of the living God brings human life eternal livingness, then the time of this eternity is no longer irreversible time. It is rather the reversible time of the circling movements which set life permanently in the mode of duration, so that we can talk about a 'life everlasting' and a 'world without end'. This is probably what Johann Rist meant with his paradox 'time without time' and 'beginning without ending'.[7] So we cannot argue that eternal life is either a perfection without life or a life that is not perfect and complete.[8] The perfection too embraces love and creative movement. If this were not so, God himself would either be perfect but without life, or living but imperfect. But it is precisely from his perfection that God's creative livingness follows. Consequently in their perfect fellowship with God human beings will also share in God's creative primality. We can therefore imagine eternal life as an inexhaustibly creative livingness. Then in all created beings the fullness of the Deity dwells bodily.

The Place of Eternal Life

'Brothers, remain true to the earth, and do not believe those who talk to you about other-worldly hopes', Friedrich Nietzsche warned his contemporaries in his *Zarathustra* (1.3). But is the place of eternal life really a heaven beyond the earth, not a heaven on this earth at all? Far from leading human beings away from earth to heaven, the Christian hope leads them to the kingdom of God which comes on earth. It is the angels who belong to heaven. Human beings have come from the earth and belong on earth, and do so in both time and eternity. If heaven opens for them, it is heaven on earth. The kingdom of God has a direct relationship to the earth. It lives with the earth, and it is only on earth that human beings can seek the kingdom of God. For on this earth stands the cross of Christ, and it is on this earth that we may expect the deliverance from evil. It is *this* transitory life which will be transformed into eternal life, it is *this* earthly life which will be raised to eternal life (1 Cor. 15.53f.). So like Nietzsche, what we hear from the promises of the gospel is: 'Brothers, remain true to the earth', for the earth is worth it. Expect the coming of God here, and do not dream yourselves into heavenly afterworlds. 'Only the person who loves the earth and God in one, can believe in the kingdom of God.'[9]

If human beings and the earth belong so indivisibly together, then with eternal life we must also expect a 'new earth', without the deadly shadows of the past but where eternal 'righteousness dwells' (2 Peter 3.13). That will be the earth's redemption. Eternal life can no more stand by itself than can the men and women to whom eternal life is to be given. It is therefore bound up with the future world.

To the soul belongs the body, so there can be no salvation for the soul without bodily resurrection. To the human being there belongs human community, so there can be no individual salvation without a new community. To the human community belongs the natural environment of the earth and its inhabitants, so there can be no salvation for human beings without the new creation of the earth and the redemption of the whole sighing and groaning creation. God the Creator remains faithful to his creation in its redemption too, and 'does not forsake the works of his hands'. He doesn't give anything up for lost, and destroys nothing he has made. That is why in the Bible the redemption is called 'new creation', and this embraces 'everything' (Rev. 21.5). Because many ideas of redemption that are hostile to creation and destructive of the world have crept into Christianity in the course of its history, this must be so much stressed, even if the images about 'the resurrection of the body' and 'the new earth' have become alien to scientific thinking in modern times. It is only the now-developing postmodern holistic and ecological thinking which these terms can once again illuminate. Then burial also acquires a deeper meaning. How would it be if at the graveside instead of saying: '. . . and *from* this earth Christ will raise you at the Last Day', we said: '. . . and *with* this earth you will be raised'? For where are the dead to be raised *to* if not the new earth?

Will the Life We Have Lived Be Preserved in Eternal Life?

Shall we be raised as the same persons we were, or shall we be different? Shall we recognize ourselves again? What happens to our identity in the deadly difference between time and eternity, mortality and immortality? So as not to answer the question in abstract terms, we may say that we 'shall be called by our names'. Our name means our whole person, and our whole biography. Neither a bodiless soul nor a soulless body can be called by this name – not even the same person in only one condition or aspect of his or her life. In the moment of eternity, the life in time that we lived in sequence, as our age advanced, will be simultaneous and will thus be transformed into eternal livingness before the face of God. So we shall recognize ourselves entirely when we hear our names. The life we have lived will be absorbed into the eternal livingness and preserved there.

But is that to lead to the eternalization of all our misdeeds and sufferings? 'Resurrection' always also means transformation (1 Cor. 15.52), the forgiveness of sins and the putting right of what was wrong, the consoling of grief and the wiping away of the tears. That is not a transformation into a different being; it is a transformation of our own being through reconciliation. Even the guilt that has been forgiven remains in the memory, though it is no longer a burden. Even wounds that have healed can still be seen from the scars they have left, though they no longer hurt. Even if the tears of grief are wiped away and the grief has been turned into joy, the eyes are still wet. By this I mean: when our temporal life is transformed into eternal livingness, that life doesn't disappear; it will be 'transfigured'. It will be accepted, put right, reconciled, sanctified and glorified. But it is still our life, just as we still remain ourselves in that life, and for the first time come properly and fully to ourselves.

It has sometimes been asked whether in eternal life all human beings are the same, and the differences between man and woman will come to an end. It is true that according to the Gospel of Matthew Jesus says (22.30): 'In the resurrection they neither marry nor are given in marriage, but are like the angels of God in heaven.' But this doesn't mean that human beings will become angels. It is a comparison. I believe that the sexual difference is part of our identity and that it therefore won't disappear. If God created human beings to be his image as male and female, then he created them in this way for eternal life as well. Eternal life is the same for all in the future world they share, but the future world is no less colourful and variegated than this first world of ours.

I don't believe that there will be there a different reward for good works or for innocent sufferings here. But through Pentecost the Christian community has already become a social place of different charismata, gifts and tasks, so how much more will the new creation of all things now created consist of an overflowing measure of charismatic powers and spiritual gifts! For the Christian community has always understood its charismatic endowment as the springtime and foretaste of the future world. Its charismatic powers are not supernatural gifts but 'the powers of the age to come' (Heb. 6.5). So 'the age to come' must itself be overflowing with such powers, so that the fullness of the eternal livingness is open to all – to each his or her own, and to all together. What must be expected is accordingly not a monotony of eternity but the many voices of the fullness of life. Only death is monotonous, not the new creation.

What Can We Know about Eternal Life?

Couldn't everything be quite different? Have I said more than anyone can say in this impaired and mortal life about the life beyond? Of course no one has ever come back and told us about it. And we all know that hopes can be disappointed, and that hope can be the fool's paradise. And yet the future of eternal life is not so completely up in the air, and not so completely without any relation to what we know, that nothing can be said about it at all from the present standpoint of this life, or that anything we say can only be speculative. I have been led to the ideas about the eternal livingness I have put forward here by three considerations:

(a) The God of Abraham, Isaac and Jacob is 'the God of hope', for he promises life and he keeps his promises. His whole being is *faithfulness*. So we can rely on his promise and trust ourselves to his word. He will therefore never let what he has created go, but will complete at the end his creation at the beginning, and will make it his eternal creation. God has created human beings for eternal life. So he will lead them to the life of his eternal presence. Neither human recalcitrance nor death can prevent him, for God is God. The eternally bounteous God is not a pedantic bookkeeper of our faults or merits, but communicates over-flowing life out of the plenitude of his goodness. His words are promises, the people he calls are prophets, his acts in history open up future, and all created life is life in its beginnings, and is hence a true promise of its future beside God, the future of eternal life.

(b) Jesus has been raised from the dead and has become the Christ of the future: the New Testament calls him the first fruit of those who have fallen asleep and the leader of life. Through his *raising from the dead*, the all-embracing prospect of the life of the future world has been opened up for the living and the dead. Where men and women perceive Christ's resurrection and begin to live within its horizon, they themselves will be born again to a living hope which reaches beyond death, and in living love will begin to experience eternal life in the fulfilled moment. They experience themselves in God, and God in themselves, and that is eternal life. The contemplation of Christ and experiences in the community of Christ are the foundations for all Christian ideas about eternal life and the future world. Christ's resurrection is not just the beginning of the Christian faith in time; it is also its eternal origin.

(c) In the community of Christ we experience *God's Spirit* as a power of life which makes us live. This is an infectious livingness which shows itself in affirmed life and new courage for living. Because in this experience of life we come close to the eternal origin of all things, these powers of life are also powers of the future world. They are powers which come into our mortal life here from the eternal life on the other side of death, and kindle the beginning of the life which reaches beyond death.

The faithfulness of God in history, Christ's resurrection, and the experience of life in God's Spirit are the grounds for the expectation of eternal life in God's future new world. We are only drawing the conclusions, and tracing the horizons of the hope which springs from these foundations. And in so doing we arrive at eternal life.

Notes

PART ONE:
THERE IS A MAGIC IN EVERY BEGINNING

I The Promise of the Child

1. E. Norden, *Die Geburt des Kindes. Geschichte einer religiösen Idee* (1924), Darmstadt, 1969.
2. Virgil, *Eclogues*, trans. H. Rushton Fairclough, revised G. P. Goold (Loeb ed.), Cambridge, Mass., and London, 1999.
3. Heraclitus, *Fragments*, trans. T. M. Robinson, Toronto, Buffalo and London, 1987.
4. 'Welch ein Gehemnis ist ein Kind!
   Gott ist auch ein Kind gewesen.
   Weil wir Gottes Kinder sind,
   kam ein Kind, uns zu erlösen.
   Welch ein Geheimnis ist ein Kind!
   Wer dies einmal je empfunden,
   ist den Kindern durch das Jesuskind verbunden.
                    (Clemens Brentano)
5. P. Ariés, *Centuries of Childhood*, trans. from French by R. Baldick, London, 1973.
6. J. Korczak, *Wie man ein Kind lieben soll*, 8th ed., Göttingen, 1983, 40.
7. G. Schimanowski, *Weisheit und Messias*, Tübingen, 1989.
8. F. Christ, *Jesus Sophia. Die Sophia-Christologie bei den Synoptikern*, Zürich, 1970.
9. Marcia J. Bunge (ed.), *The Child in Christian Thought*, Grand Rapids, 2001.
10. M. Montessori, *The Secret of Childhood*, trans. from Italian by B. Barclay Carter, London and New York, 1936.
11. E. Bloch, *Das Prinzip Hoffnung*, Frankfurt, 1959, 1628 (*The Principle of Hope*, trans. N. and S. Plaice and P. Knight, Cambridge, Mass., and Oxford, 1986).

12. E. Bloch, *Geist der Utopie*, 1918, 2nd ed. 1923 (reprint Frankfurt, 1964, 246 (*The Spirit of Utopia*, trans. A. Nassar, Stanford, Ca., 2000).

II *Does the Future Belong to the Young?*

1. Time present and time past
   are both perhaps present in time future,
   and time future contained in time past.
                                    (T. S. Eliot, *Burnt Norton*)
   See also J. Moltmann, *God in Creation* (the Gifford Lectures 1984–85), trans. Margaret Kohl, London and New York, 1985, Ch. V.5: The Interlaced Times of History, 124ff.
2. H. Blüher, *Wandervogel – Geschichte einer Jugendbewegung*, 3 vols, Berlin, 1912.
3. H. Giesecke, *Vom Wandervogel bis zur Hitlerjugend. Jugendarbeit zwischen Politik und Pädagogik*, Munich, 1981.
4. The two countries which have not ratified the United Nations Convention on the Rights of Children (1989) are the United States and Somalia.
5. D. Walsh, *Selling out America's Children. How America puts Profits before Values – and what Parents can do*, Minneapolis, 1994.

PART TWO: IN MY END IS MY BEGINNING

III *New Beginnings in Catastrophes*

1. C. Westermann, *Genesis 1–11. A Commentary*, trans. J. J. Scullion, Minneapolis, 1984, 416.
2. Elaine Pagels, *Adam, Eve, and the Serpent*, New York and London, 1988, 42ff.
3. F. Delitzsch, quoted in Westermann, *Genesis 1–11*, 408.
4. Delitzsch, quoted in Westermann, *Genesis 1–11*, 408.
5. Westermann, *Genesis 1–11*, 394.
6. H. Donner, *Geschichte des Volkes Israel und seiner Nachbarn in Grundzügen*, vol. II, 2nd ed., Göttingen, 1995, 402ff.
7. B. Janowski, *Gottes Gegenwart in Israel*, Neukirchen, 1993.
8. Gershom Scholem, 'Zum Verständnis der messianischen Idee im Judentum', *Judaica* 1, Frankfurt, 1963, 7–74.
9. J. Moltmann, 'Resurrection: The Ground, Power and Goal of our Hope', *Concilium*, 1999/5, 81–9.
10. *Apocrypha and Pseudepigrapha of the Old Testament in English*, ed. R. H. Charles, Oxford, 1963, vol. 2.

IV Deliver Us from Evil

1. Cf. Supplement 10, *ZThK*, December 1998, and there especially D. Wendebourg, 'Zur Entstehungsgeschichte der "Gemeinsame Erklärung"', 140–206.
2. Cf. W. E. Gladstone (1809–1898), speaking of Ireland: 'I tremble for my country when I remember that God is just.' I am indebted to Margaret Kohl for drawing my attention to this quotation.
3. Or rather:

   Wir wären gut anstatt so roh,
   doch die Verhältnisse, die sind nicht so.

   (Bert Brecht, *Die Dreigroschenoper*)

   For the English translation see Kurt Weill, *The Threepenny Opera*, ed. S. Hinton, Cambridge, 1990.
4. B. Janowski, 'Der Barmherzige Richter. Zur Einheit von Gerechtigkeit und Barmherzigkeit im Gottesbild des Alten Orient und des Alten-Testaments', in R. Scoralick (ed.), *Das Drama der Barmherzigkeit. Studien zur biblischen Gottesrede und ihrer Wirkungsgeschichte in Judentum und Christentum,* Stuttgart, 2000, 33–91. Cf. also J. Assmann et al. (eds), *Gerechtigkeit. Richten und Retten in der abendländischen Tradition und ihren altorientalischen Ursprüngen,* Munich, 1988.
5. This was maintained with great clarity by J. H. Iwand in 'Glaubens-gerechtigkeit nach Luthers Lehre', *Theologische Existenz heute,* Heft 75, Munich, 1941.
6. For more detail here see J. Moltmann, *The Way of Jesus Christ. Christology in Messianic Dimensions,* trans. Margaret Kohl, London and San Francisco, 1990, esp. Ch. III, The Messianic Mission of Christ, 73–150.
7. Ernst Bloch, *Das Prinzip Hoffnung,* Frankfurt, 1959, 1490,1495 (*The Principle of Hope,* trans. N. and S. Plaice and P. Knight, Cambridge, Mass., and Oxford, 1986).
8. In the original, this verse from 'O Haupt voll Blut und Wunden' runs as follows:

   Wenn ich einmal soll scheiden,
   dann scheide nicht von mir.
   Wenn ich den Tod soll leiden,
   so tritt du dann herfür;
   wenn mir am allerbängsten
   wird um das Herze sein,
   dann reiss mich aus den Ängsten
   kraft deiner Angst und Pein.
9. Christ's solidarity with us in our fear is not brought out in the familiar

translation 'O sacred head, sore wounded'. But what Paul Gerhardt actually wrote was: 'Snatch me out of my *fears* through thy *fear* and suffering.'

10. Cf. D. Bonhoeffer, *Letters and Papers from Prison*, ed. E. Bethge, trans. R. H. Fuller, (4th) enlarged ed., London and New York, 1971, 361 (letter of 16 July 1944).

11. On the question of God's co-suffering or his impassibility, see Karl Rahner's dispute with me and mine with him in J. Moltmann, *History and the Triune God. Contributions to Trinitarian Theology*, trans. J. Bowden, London and Philadelphia, 1991, 122–4.

12. J. Sobrino, 'Oscar Arnulfo Romero, Märtyrer der Befreiung' in J. Sobrino (ed.), *Romero, die Notwendige Revolution*, German trans. from the Spanish by E. Págan, Munich and Mainz, 1982, 17.

13. 'In illo vera mors facta est, sic in nobis vera remissio peccatorum, quemadmodum in illo vera resurrectio, ita in nobis vera justificatio' ('In that very same sense in which death is real, so also is the forgiveness of our sins real, and in the same sense in which his resurrection is real, so also in us is there authentic justification' [Augustine, *Enchiridion*, 52, trans. A. C. Outler, London, 1955]).

14. Thus R. Bultmann in 'The New Testament and Mythology' in *Kerygma and Dogma*, ed. H. W. Bartsch, trans. R. H. Fuller, London, 1960, 41: 'Faith in the resurrection is really the same thing as faith in the saving efficacy of the cross.'

15. K. Barth, *Church Dogmatics*, Edinburgh, 1958, IV/1, § 59.

16. H. J. Iwand, 'Glaubensgerechtigkeit nach Luthers Lehre', *Theologische Existenz heute*, Heft 75, Munich, 1941, 11: Gott recht geben, Glaube und erstes Gebot.

17. E. Bloch, *Geist der Utopie*, 1918, 2nd ed. 1923, reprint Frankfurt, 1964, 346 (*The Spirit of Utopia*, trans. A. Nassar, Stanford, Ca., 2000).

V *The Spirituality of the Wakeful Senses*

1. On the concept of 'numbing', cf. Robert J. Lifton, *The Life of the Self. Toward a New Psychology*, New York, 1976, and G. Müller-Fahrenholz, *Erwecke die Welt. Unser Glaube an Gottes Geist in dieser bedrohten Zeit*, Gütersloh, 1997, 78–111.

2. *The Collected Wisdom of Heraclitus*, trans. Brooks Haxton, New York and London, 2001 (Fragment 89).

VI *The Living Power of Hope*

1. See J. Moltmann, *Theology of Hope*, trans. J. W. Leitch, London, 1967; many later editions, lastly SCM Classics, London, 2002, with a new preface by Richard Bauckham.

2. L. Ragaz, *Der Kampf um das Reich Gottes in Blumhardt, Vater und Sohn – und weiter!*, Zürich, 1922, 157.

3. *Hegel's Philosophy of Right*, trans. T. M. Knox, London, 1947, Preface, 12–13.

4. J. Calvin, *In omnes Novi Testamenti Epistolas Commentarii*, vol. II, Halle, 1834, 484.

5. W. Rauschenbusch, *Christianizing the Social Order*, New York, 1912.

6. It was to this life that the World Council of Churches called at its assembly in Uppsala in 1968: 'We ask you, trusting in God's renewing power, to join in the anticipation of God's Kingdom, already showing now something of the newness whch Christ will complete on his day.'

PART THREE: O BEGINNING WITHOUT ENDING . . .

1. Among German poets, Hermann Hesse took up this theme:

Es wird vielleicht auch noch die Todesstunde
Uns neuen Räumen jung entgegensenden.
Des Lebens Ruf wird niemals enden . . .
Wohlan denn, Herz nimm Abschied und gesunde.

2. 'O Ewigkeit, Zeit ohne Zeit,
O Anfang sonder Ende . . .'

VII Is There a Life After Death?

1. W. Biermann, *Preussischer Ikarus. Lieder, Balladen, Gedichte, Prosa.*, Cologne, 1978, 93.

2. See Plato, *Phaedo*.

3. *The Bhagavad-Gita*, trans. and ed. by R. C. Zaehner, Oxford, 1969, II, 20, 11, 15, 17.

4. H. Sonnemans, *Seele. Unsterblichkeit – Auferstehung*, Freiburg, 1984.

5. Paul Gerhardt expresses the same idea but, unlike Caswell, with confident vigour rather than resignation:

Kann uns doch kein Tod nicht töten,
sondern reißt
unsern Geist
aus vielen tausend Nöten.

6. Charles Hartshorne, *The Logic of Perfection*, London, 1963.

7. J. Ratzinger, *Eschatology: death and eternal life*, trans. M. Waldstein, translation edited by Aidan Nichols, Washington, D.C., 1988.

8. See Chapter IV.4 below.

9. Poem translated directly from the German.

10. J. Le Goff, *The Birth of Purgatory*, trans. from French by A. Goldhammer, London 1984.

11. M. Luther, *Smalcald Articles*, Part II, Article 2.
12. P. Althaus, *Die letzten Dinge*, 7th ed., Gütersloh, 1957.
13. R. Hummel, *Reinkarnation, Weltbilder des Reinkarnationsglaubens und des Christentum*, Stuttgart, 1988.
14. In Shakespeare's *Twelfth Night* the question has even made its way into high comedy:

> CLOWN: What is the opinion of Pythagoras concerning wild fowl?
> MALVOLIO: That the soul of our grandam might haply inhabit a bird.
> CLOWN: What thinkest thou of his opinion?
> MALVOLIO: I think nobly of the soul, and no way approve his opinion.
>
> (Act IV, scene 2)

15. *The Bhagavad-Gita*, trans. and ed. by R. C. Zaehner, Oxford, 1969, II, 22.
16. H. Quistorp, *Die letzten Dinge im Zeugnis Calvins*, Gütersloh, 1941, 79–91.

VIII Mourning and Consoling

1. E. Jüngel, *Death: the riddle and the mystery*, trans. I. and U. Nichol, Edinburgh, 1975.
2. C. Lasch, *The Culture of Narcissism. American Life in an Age of Diminishing Experience*, New York, 1978.
3. D. Bonhoeffer, *Letters and Papers from Prison*, ed. E. Bethge, trans. R. H. Fuller, et al., enlarged edition, London, 1971, 176: letter of Christmas Eve 1943 (trans. slightly altered).
4. S. Kahl-Passoth et al., *Nimmt das denn nie ein Ende? Mit Trauer leben lernen*, Gütersloh, 1992.
5. S. Freud, 'Mourning and Melancholia', trans. J. Riviere, in *Collected Papers of Sigmund Freud*, IV, London, 1925, 152–70.
6. T. Rees, *Hymns and Psalms*, Methodist Publishing House, 1983, No. 36, verse 2. We may also again remember Paul Gerhardt's verse in 'O sacred head sore wounded': And when my heart must languish / Amidst the final throe, / Release my from mine anguish / by thine own pain and woe ('Wenn mir am allerbängsten / wird um das Herze sein, / dan reiss mich aus den Ängsten, / kraft deiner Angst und Pein'), see above pp. 70, 167.

IX The Community of the Living and the Dead

1. Lee, Jung-Young (ed.), *Ancestor Worship and Christianity in Korea*, New York, 1988.

Notes

2. R. van Gulik, *The Chinese Nail Murders*, London, 1961, Panther ed. 1966, 152f.
3. Yu, Hong-rkol, *Geschichte der katholischen Kirche in Korea*, Seoul, 1994, 97.

X *What Awaits Us?*

1. A. Champdor, *Das ägyptische Totenbuch*, Munich, 1980, 84: 'But above all they appear without fear before the Lord of righteousness and truth in the divine tribunal . . . They will have to put forward their justification as all the dead have had to do since the beginning of the world in the course of that dreadful testing which awaits them: the weighing of the soul', the psychostasis.
2. T. Moser, *Gottesvergiftung*, Hamburg, 1976.
3. No. 1037. Cf. also the statement by the Doctrine Commission of the Church of England, *The Mystery of Salvation*, London, 1995, 198–9: 'Nevertheless it is our conviction that the reality of hell (and indeed of heaven) is the ultimate affirmation of the reality of human freedom.'
4. M. Wolf, 'The Final Reconciliation. Reflections on the Social Dimension of the Eschatological Transition', *Modern Theology* 16 (2000), 91–113.
5. L. Ragaz, *Der Kampf um das Reich Gottes in Blumhardt, Vater und Sohn – und weiter!*, Zürich, 1922, 153.
6. See *The Book of Concord, The Confessions of the Evangelical Lutheran Church*, trans. and ed. T. G. Tappert, Philadelphia, 1959, 38. So too the Confessio Helvetica Posterior (1566), Article XI.
7. M. Luther, Sermon on Preparing for Death (1519), WA 2, 691.
8. C. Wesley, 'Christ the Lord is risen today'.
9. H. Urs von Balthasar, *Kleiner Diskurs über die Hölle*, Ostfildern, 1987.
10. Christian Fürchtegott Gellert (1715–69):

    Jesus lebt! Ich bin gewiss, nichts soll mich von Jesus scheiden,
    keine Macht der Finsternis, keine Herrlichkeit, kein Leiden.

11. See J. Moltmann, 'The Tortured Christ' in *Jesus Christ for Today's World*, trans. Margaret Kohl, London and Minneapolis, 1994, 58–70.
12. See D. Bonhoeffer, *Letters and Papers from Prison*, ed. R. Bethge, trans. R. H. Fuller et al., enlarged ed., London and New York, 1971, 169–170: letter to Bethge of 18 December 1943. Bonhoeffer is commenting on some lines in Paul Gerhardt's Christmas hymn 'Fröhlich soll mein Herze springen':

    Lasst fahr'n, O liebe Brüder,
    was euch fehlt,
    was euch quält,
    Ich bring' alles wieder.

13. F. Groth, *Die 'Wiederbringung aller Dinge' im württembergischen Pietismus*, Göttingen, 1984.

XI *Eternal Life*

1. This was finely stressed by P. Althaus in his article 'Ewiges Leben IV. dogmatisch' in RGG³, II, 805–9, Cf. also H. Küng, *Eternal Life?*, trans. E. Quinn, London, 1984.
2. This 'Drunken Song' from *Also sprach Zarathustra'* is engraved on a stone on the peninsula Chaste near Sils Maria.
3. E. Bloch, *Spuren*, Frankfurt, 1959, 7.
4. B. Groethuysen, *Philosophische Anthropologie*, Munich and Berlin, 1928, 7, almost in the same words as Ernst Bloch later.
5. M. Scheler, *Die Stellung des Menschen im Kosmos*, Munich, 1949, 56, who concludes from the human being's 'emptiness of heart' the 'elevation to openness to the world' which goes beyond all frontiers.
6. M. Grabmann, *Die Grundgedanken des Heiligen Augustinus über Seele und Gott*, Darmstadt, 1957; H. Scholz, *Fruitio Dei. Ein Beitrag zur Geschichte der Theologie und der Mystik*, Leipzig, 1911.
7. Johann Rist (1607–67). See Part Three note 2 above.
8. F. Schleiermacher, *The Christian Faith*, trans. H. R. Mackintosh and J. S. Stewart from the 2nd ed., Edinburgh, 1928, reprint Philadelphia, 1976, §§ 159, 163.
9. D. Bonhoeffer, 'Dein Reich komme' (1932), Hamburg, 1958. Cf. L. Ragaz, *Der Kampf um das Reich Gottes in Blumhardt, Vater und Sohn – und weiter!*, Zürich, 1922, 55–61.

Earlier Publications Relating to the Subjects Treated Here

1. 'Kind und Kindheit als Metaphern der Hoffnung', *EvTh* 60/2, 92–102. Lecture in the framework of the Studium Generale of the University of Tübingen on 25 January 1999.

2. 'Apokalyptische Katastrophentheologie' in *Katastrophe – Trauma oder Erneuerung?*, Tübingen, 2001, 25–40. Lecture in a series on catastrophe medicine, Tübingen 2 May 2000.

3. 'Die Rechtfertigung Gottes', *Stimmen der Zeit*, vol. 219/7, 435–42; 219/8, 507–19, and in R. Weth (ed.), *Das Kreuz Jesu. Gewalt – Opfer – Sühne*, Neukirchen, 2001, 120–42. Lecture at the biennial conference of the Gesellschaft für Evangelische Theologie in Münster on 20 February 2001.

4. 'Gibt es ein Leben nach dem Tod?', lecture at the Evangelischer Kirchentag in Stuttgart on 18 June 1999, in K. von Bonin and A. Gidion (eds), *Deutscher Evangelischer Kirchentag Stuttgart 1999*, Gütersloh, 1999, 296–309.

5. 'Death, Mourning and Consolation' in *The Coming of God. Christian Eschatology*, trans. Margaret Kohl, London and Minneapolis, 1996, 119–28.

Index

childhood, ambiguities of, 6,
   8; class dimension, 6–7;
   innocence, 10, 14; of Jesus,
   4–5; perspectives on, 6–10
children, in ancient world, 12;
   as consumers, 26; of God,
   77; as God's promise,
   16–18; Jesus and, 12–15;
   mysticism of, 16; rights of,
   8;
Christology, of
   representation, 71–4; of
   solidarity, 69–70
Chrysostom, John, 93
Communist Manifesto, 23
Confucius, 11
consumerism, 25
courage, 31
covenant, Noachic, 36–41;
   reconception of, 43
crucifixion, as catastrophe,
   45; as solidarity, 69–71, 74;
   as world's answer, 69

Darwin, Charles, 145
death, 65, 99, 101–2, 119–20;
   mourning, 122–9; prayer
   about, 136–7; repression of,
   121–2; remembrance of the
   dead, 137–8; rituals of,
   120–1, 136; *see also* life
   after death, eternal life
descent into hell, 148–9
despair, 93–5

Einstein, Albert, 34
Eliot, T. S., xi, 166
Emerson, Ralph Waldo, 15
eschatology, xii, 47
eternal life, as new livingness,

152–4,159; identity in,
   161–2; meaning, of, 152–3;
   time and place of, 159–61;
   see also life after death
evil, 31, 37, 48, 53–4, 56–1;
   see also victims;
   perpetrators
exile, Israel's, 41–4
expiation, 73, 110–11, 115,
   117; *see also* perpetrators;
   purgatory

faith, 66–7
Flood story, 18, 31, 36–41
Fra Angelico, 80
Frank, Hans, 138
Fredrick the Great, 152
Freud, Sigmund, 125–7, 128
friend-enemy thinking, xii, 25
future; hope for, 87, 88; in
   traditional societies, 20;
   symbols of, 4; and youth,
   20–1, 27

Galatians, Letter to the, 72
Genesis sagas;
   Abraham/Sarah, 3, 11;
   Moses, 155–6; Noah and
   flood, 36–41, 73
Gerhard, Paul, 70
global warming, 82
God, and catastrophes, 38–9,
   43; contemplation of,
   156–9; indwelling, 43–4,
   63, 155, 158; justice of, 57,
   61–3; and life, xii; mutual
   indwelling with, 16, 158–9;
   question of, 34–5; presence
   of, 16, 63; suffering of, 39,
   41, 63, 70–1, 73–4,